YALE LANGUAGE SERIES

# The French Correction

## Correction

Grammatical Problems for
Review and Reference

**NORMAN SUSSKIND**

**YALE UNIVERSITY PRESS**
New Haven and London

Designed by Nancy Ovedovitz and set in VIP Meridien type by Eastern Typesetting. Printed in the United States of America by Murray Printing Company, Westford, Massachusetts.

**Library of Congress Cataloging in Publication Data**

Susskind, Norman, 1929–
    The French correction.
    Includes index.
    1. French language—Grammar—1950–   . 2. French language—Textbooks for foreign speakers—English.
I. Title.
PC2112.S97  1984    448.2′421      83–23530
ISBN 0–300–03157–2
ISBN 0–300–03158–0 (pbk)

The paper in this book meets the guidelines for permanence and durability of the Committee on Production Guidelines for Book Longevity of the Council on Library Resources.

10    9    8    7    6    5

# Contents

# Preface

Some parts of French grammar continue to trouble even the best students throughout their advanced courses in the subject—and often well beyond, into real-life use of the language. In this little book I have isolated a dozen of those points and have devoted a full chapter to each, hoping, by thoroughness or cunning, finally to exorcise the demons.

My choice of topics was far from arbitrary. More than twenty-five years of university teaching are behind it. Of course, not everyone will agree with all the inclusions and exclusions. Some will surely say: "How could he leave out the subtropical invective, or the insipid plupervert, or the connubial ablution?" or whatever. The fact is that there's no clear stopping place. This book is unique in that it *does* reflect a choice, one made with an eye not to the myriad beginners but to the relatively small number of those who can, perhaps with some hesitation, answer "Yes" to the question "Do you speak French?" The concentrated instruction and review of specific problems offered here will help you to keep that an honest answer.

Being an American who learned French in American schools, I think I have a pretty good understanding of the problems that beset you as you strive for fluency. And, being an American, I have chosen to use English as the basic language here for instruction and comment. That permits me to be more subtle and to give

more thorough and inventive explanations than would be prac-
ticable if we worked together entirely in French.

Pensée number 29 of Pascal is:

> Quand on voit le style naturel, on est tout étonné et ravi,
> car on s'attendait de voir un auteur et on trouve un homme.

Pascal probably didn't have this book in mind when he wrote that,
but it has influenced me anyway. In a long teaching career, I have
seldom seen "un homme" behind a textbook. Authors of grammars—usually committees—try very hard not to appear to exist,
to be altogether impersonal, which greatly enhances the soporific
potential of most texts. So to aspire to write the world's most
amusing French grammar was not as outrageous as it might seem.
So, too, you will sometimes find "un homme"—not to say a wise
guy—grinning or even leering up at you from these pages.

Please, though, be not deceived by the quips, the sallies, the bon-
homie; my purpose is serious. In fact, the book is quite dense and
should be perused slowly. I have employed a system of three-digit
reference numbers in the margins throughout the text and have
used them in the index instead of page numbers to refer you quickly
to specifics of grammar or to help you find the answers to individual
questions, but for the most part the chapters are organic wholes,
and you should read them as units. The discussions generally go
far beyond those in customary grammars, and only a near-path-
ological modesty prevents me from saying that they are also more
lucid.

It remains to offer heartfelt thanks to Monique Pitts, who helped
purge my text of unfrenchnesses, and to Sally Dayner, who did
the drawings.

And last—perhaps a word of gratitude to Caesar's legions and to
the Vandals, Visigoths, Celts, Franks, Gauls, and to their many
millions of descendants, for their role in making the French language. They might have made it a little easier, but I guess they did
the best they could. In any case, this book owes its existence to
them.

# 1 ○ **Articles**

001 The French indefinite article causes no problems for American students, and so it can be safely omitted from this discussion.* You couldn't possibly have gotten this far in language study without understanding how to use it.

The definite and partitive articles, on the other hand, do cause some confusion. Happily, as you are about to learn, that can be resolved with ridiculous ease.

002 **MARKING OF NOUNS**

Remember that French nearly always marks, or introduces, nouns. This is done by:

- an article
  definite          Tu connais *la* femme.
  indefinite        Tu connais *une* femme.
  partitive         Tu connais *des* femmes.
- a possessive adjective    Vous portez *mes* livres.
- a demonstrative           Je préfère *ce* tableau-ci.
- sometimes a number        Elle a vu *36 mille* chandelles.
- a preposition             Il lit *avec* soin.

In English, this is not always the case. Here are some examples of unmarked nouns:

*Q. Why is a French omelet never made with two eggs?
A. Because in France one egg is un oeuf.

**1**

I got shoes.
Roses are red.
Ask questions.
She sells sea shells.
We love spinach.

We will concern ourselves here only with the definite and partitive articles. The other markers, with an inconsequential exception or two (well, maybe three), are used just as they are in English. The only problem arises where English has no marker at all. Then we must decide between the definite and the partitive in French.

003 **THE DEFINITE ARTICLE**

The definite article has two functions in French. First, it may indicate that the noun following is to be taken in a general sense. The sentences "Roses are red" and "We love spinach," which are general statements, would be *"Les* roses sont rouges" and "Nous aimons *les* épinards." They refer not to certain roses or to a particular batch of spinach, but to roses and spinach *in general.* Further examples are:

J'essaie d'éviter *le* poison.
*Les* violettes sont bleues.
Pourquoi trouves-tu *la* chimie barbante?
*Les* chiens ne parlent pas trop.
*Le* cinéma prend sa place parmi les arts.

The other function of the definite article, and this applies to both French and English, is to indicate all of a quantity that is specified or limited, or whose limitation is suggested somewhere in the context. That sounds terribly complicated, but look at these illustrations:

Où sont les crayons que j'ai achetés hier?
Le vin blanc de 1915 n'est plus buvable.

In the first sentence, the speaker does not inquire about pencils in general. Rather, he inquires about *all* those that he bought yesterday (and *only* those). In the second, the statement applies not to white wine in general, but to *all* (and *only*) the white wine made in 1915. See? The context limits the quantity. We might say that the French definite article always indicates a generality, sometimes unlimited, sometimes limited.

Anyway, it is always true of the second, limited application that an equivalent English sentence would have the word **the**. We can make it even simpler: anytime English would have **the**, French calls for the definite article.

So there are two easy rules for use of the definite article in French. For the sake of order, logic, and public morality, let's call them 1 and 2.

1. Use the definite article when the utterance is an unlimited generalization.
2. Use the definite article when the utterance is a limited generalization in which **the** *would be used in English.*

The italicized part of rule 2 doesn't demonstrate any real understanding of French usage, but it's brief and it works all the time, so leave us not quibble.

Note the uses of the definite articles in this passage. They are marked with a 1 or a 2, depending on which rule applies.

Hier, la² cuisinière a acheté un kilo de beurre. Cela m'a plu, car j'aime beaucoup le¹ beurre. Elle a mis le² beurre sur la² table avant de sortir de la² cuisine. J'ai pris le² beurre et je l'ai mangé. Je peux résister à presque toutes les¹ tentations, mais le¹ beurre est trop délicieux.

Aujourd'hui je suis terriblement malade. C'est sans doute à cause du² beurre que j'ai volé. La² cuisinière n'aurait pas dû le laisser comme ça. C'est sa faute! Les¹ cuisinières ont des responsabilités, n'est-ce pas?

## 004 THE PARTITIVE ARTICLE

The partitive article, as its name suggests, is a way of referring to *part* of something; not to a generality or to a totality, which are the functions of the definite article. Look at the last sentence of the butter story: "Les cuisinières ont des responsabilités, n'est-ce pas?" It does make a general statement about cooks, but not about responsibilities. A general statement about responsibilities might be "Les responsabilités sont ennuyeuses" or "Il évite les responsabilités."

Cooks don't have responsibilities *in general;* they have *some* of them. The article **des** in that sentence is partitive.

Here are some more examples:

Les vaches sont des animaux à cornes.
All cows are horned animals, but not all horns are on cows.

Les autobus émettent du soufre.
All buses emit sulphur, but not all sulphur comes from buses.

Il y a des calories dans le sucre.
All sugar has calories, but not all calories are in sugar.

Les tigres ont des griffes.
Les pays méditerranéens produisent des oranges.

And so on.

005  Here, in summary, are some bite-size guides for use of the articles:

Use the *definite* article:

1. When making a broad generalization, as in

   Le lait est blanc.

2. When mentioning all of some quantity specified in the context—a limited generalization—as in

   Le lait que vous gardez depuis 1953 est vert.

Remember that another, easier way of stating rule 2 is that the definite article is called for in French whenever an equivalent English sentence would have **the.**

Use the *partitive* article:

1. When indicating a part (quantitatively unspecified) of some

totality, as in

Il a mangé du fromage.
Tu as de la chance.
Avez-vous trouvé de l'argent?

2. When English might, without changing the meaning, use the words **some** or **any**. This is just another way of saying what already appears in rule 1. The same examples apply. Check them if you like. (See? Maybe next time you'll trust me.)

It is not possible to dream up a set of individual sentences in which there would be a clear choice between articles. Usually both are grammatically acceptable. One is made more likely than the other by context. For instance, you would probably choose the partitive in the isolated sentence, "J'ai de l'argent dans ma poche." But in the context—"Il m'a prêté cinq dollars. J'ai l'argent dans ma poche"—the definite becomes a better choice.

Fortunately, only in grammar books and mental hospitals do people say things like, "My grandmother, a weightlifter for the CIA, pulls a rickshaw at night in spite of chocolate mousse." Life usually presents us with more coherent contexts.

Here are some sentences which, in isolation, seem to call for the partitive. In some contexts, however, the definite becomes much more likely:

Les dictionnaires contiennent *des* mots.
*but*
Les dictionnaires contiennent *les* mots acceptés et courants.

Nous avons bu *du* vin blanc.
*but*
Il ne nous restait que deux bouteilles. Nous avons mis le vin rouge dans la cave, et nous avons bu *le* vin blanc pendant la soirée.

Les pays méditerranéens produisent *des* oranges.
*but*
Les pays méditerranéens produisent *les* oranges que je préfère.

Notre atmosphère contient *de* l'oxygène.

*but*

> Notre atmosphère contient l'oxygène dont les plantes et les animaux ont besoin.

> Il a mis *des* diamants dans cette boîte.

*but*

> Après avoir commis *le* vol chez Tiffany, il a mis *les* diamants dans cette boîte et les rubis dans un sac.

As you know, things happen to the partitive when it is used in the negative, in expressions of quantity, or before plural adjectives. This is a simple, mechanical matter, and it is beneath my dignity to mention it, but I'm throwing in this reminder anyway, as a gesture of goodwill. For example:

> Il n'apporte pas de livres.
> Il apporte beaucoup de livres.
> Il apporte de beaux livres.

Note that in each case, the partitive is reduced to its first component, the preposition **de.**

006   One more small item. As always, there are some special cases that don't appear to fit the overall pattern. They have to be learned separately. Such cases are the French use of the definite article in the sense of **per,** where English usually has the indefinite **a** or **an.** This is particularly true of prices.

> Cinquante francs la bouteille.
> Six francs le kilo.

007   Also, with nouns of time, where English might use **every.**

> L'été je pars en vacances.
> Le matin il prend une douche.
> Le lundi elle va en classe.

These cases don't fit clearly under the "general statement" heading. I could try to present them that way, but you'd probably remain unconvinced. So just learn them as a couple of oddities. No big deal.

# 2 ∘ **Object Pronouns**

**FORMS**

Somewhere in a rectangular nook, cranny, or recess of your brain, stash this rectangular schema of the pronouns. It starts with the subjects and then gives corresponding forms of the different kinds of objects:

| Person | Subject | Direct Object | Indirect Object | Disjunctive Emphatic | Reflexive |
|--------|---------|---------------|-----------------|----------------------|-----------|
| 1 sing. | je | me | me | moi | me |
| 2 sing. | tu | te | te | toi | te |
| 3 sing. masc. | il | le | lui | lui | se |
| 3 sing. fem. | elle | la | lui | elle | se |
| 1 plur. | nous | nous | nous | nous | nous |
| 2 plur. | vous | vous | vous | vous | vous |
| 3 plur. masc. | ils | les | leur | eux | se |
| 3 plur. fem. | elles | les | leur | elles | se |

Don't despair. Look at the bright side: **nous** and **vous** are always **nous** and **vous.** Also, several of the forms are the same for both masculine and feminine. It could have been worse.

7

That's our raw material. Now we must look at each kind of object and understand its use.

009 **DIRECT OBJECT PRONOUNS**

These are the objects of transitive verbs. They are *directly* affected by the action.

> Georges a besoin de son râtelier, mais il *le* perd souvent.
> Où est la bouteille? *La* vide-t-elle?
> Nos enfants *nous* tracassent.
> Les fenêtres? Oui, il *les* a ouvertes.
> Aimez-vous Brahms? Moi, je *l'*adore.
> Le président *te* connaît?

010 **INDIRECT OBJECT PRONOUNS**

These are the objects of intransitive verbs. There *is* an intermediary preposition—expressed with noun objects, implicit in pronouns.

Look. If you can fabriculate a sergle, then the sergle is a direct object, the direct recipient of the fabriculation. But if you must fabriculate *to* a sergle, then it is an indirect object. For example:

*Noun object:*                          *Pronoun object:*
Il rend visite aux voisins.             Il leur rend visite.
Je donne de la monnaie au               Je lui donne de la monnaie.
mendiant.

Please remember that many verbs can be either transitive or intransitive; they can take both kinds of objects. In the sentence "Je donne des livres à mon fils," the things you are giving, the direct objects, are the books. The person *to* whom you are giving them, the indirect object, is your son. Consider also:

> Faites attention (*direct*) au conférencier (*indirect*).
> Jetons les perles (*direct*) aux cochons (*indirect*).

Most often, transitive and intransitive verbs are the same ones in French and English, but there are a few important differences you must learn:

| *English indirect:* | *French direct:* |
|---|---|
| A cat can look *at* a king. | Un chat peut regarder un roi. |
| Listen *to* the nightingale. | Ecoutez le rossignol. |
| What are you looking *for?* | Que cherches-tu? |
| She asks *for* the moon. | Elle demande la lune. |

| *English direct:* | *French indirect:* |
|---|---|
| We obey the law. | Nous obéissons *à* la loi. |
| The meal pleased the guests. | Le repas a plu *aux* invités. |
| The girl phones her friends. | La fille téléphone *à* ses amies. |

011    And then there's the business of the verb **manquer,** sometimes referred to as the "manquer business." When the verb **manquer** is used transitively, its object is missed as a bus or a target is missed.

> Il est arrivé trop tard; il a manqué son train.
> Les flèches de Robin des Bois ne manquent jamais leur but.

Here's the challenging part: the indirect object of **manquer** is one who misses (in the sense of "feels the absence of") another. A Frenchman rarely says, literally, "I missed my wife." (No, it's not what you're thinking.) He does say "Ma femme me manquait," literally, "My wife was lacking to me." A better translation might be "I regretted my wife's absence," or, to come full circle, "I missed my wife."

"J'ai manqué ma femme" makes sense only if you threw something at her and missed or arrived too late to meet her.

A missing *thing* is referred to using the impersonal **il** as subject.

> Il manque trois boutons au manteau.
> Il manquait une fourchette au couvert.

Something needed may be designated in the same way:

> Il lui manque encore un an et il aura fini ses études.


## Y AND EN

These don't fit neatly into the rectangle. They aren't really personal, but they do function as object pronouns.

012  **Y** never stands for a person. (There are a few people I won't stand
for either, but that's a different story.) One thing **y** does is represent
a place *to* or *in* which:

Je vais en ville.                        J'y vais.
La clé est sous le paillasson.           Vous l'y trouverez.

In its other pronominal use, **y** replaces **à** + object, as long as that
object is neither human nor personified.

Je crois à la fraternité.                J'y crois.
Elle réfléchit à ses péchés.             Elle y réfléchit.

*but*

Parlez-vous aux fleurs?                   Leur parlez-vous? (Flowers
                                          personified.)

013  According to rules enforced when I was a student, **en** isn't supposed to stand for people either, but it does, particularly in familiar
discourse. Use it personally when that proves handy, but do so
sparingly.

In a way, **en** is the opposite of **y**. The latter represents a place *to*
or *in* which, a destination or location, whereas **en** represents a
place *from* which, a source.

Elle vient de Londres.                   Elle en vient.
Les bateaux partent du Havre.            Les bateaux en partent.

Broadly stated, the pronominal function of **en** is to replace **de** +
object.

Parle-t-il de ses aventures?             En parle-t-il?
Rien ne vous empêche de partir.          Rien ne vous en empêche.

**En** stands for a noun preceded by the partitive article. That's consistent; the partitive begins with the preposition **de**.

Il a commandé du café.                   Il en a commandé.
J'achète des oeufs.                      J'en achète.

Specify the quantity by adding a number or a quantitative word or expression. (Words like a cup, a spoonful, a can, a flock may be used quantitatively.)

Il a commandé une tasse de café.     Il en a commandé une tasse.
J'achète une douzaine d'oeufs.       J'en achète une douzaine.

In English, the quantitative expression may be enough by itself, as long as the substance in question is made clear somewhere in the context. A perfectly normal bit of dialogue:

— Has he any friends?
— Yes, he has a lot.

In French, **en** standing for the partitive + noun would have to be expressed in the answer.

— A-t-il des amis?
— Oui, il *en* a beaucoup.

— How many eggs did you eat?
— I ate three.

— Combien d'oeufs as-tu mangés?
— J'*en* ai mangé trois.

In this application, **en** is like "of it" or "of them."

014   **PLACEMENT OF OBJECT PRONOUNS**

Except for the affirmative imperative ("Faites-le!"), the pronoun object of a verb must come immediately before that verb.

Je ne la cherche pas.
On y va?
Nous leur obéissons.

When there are two verbs, one of them will be in the infinitive. Object pronouns usually go before the infinitive, but the real criterion is this: Object pronouns go before the verb *whose objects they are.* I couldn't come up with a way to state that more clearly. Look at the examples:

Je voudrais les voir.
("Les" is clearly the object of "voir." I'd like *to see them*.)

On commence à nous comprendre.
("Nous" is clearly the object of "comprendre." They're beginning *to understand us*.)

Elle me parle de partir.
("Me" is clearly the object of "parle." She *talks to me* about leaving.)

In compound tenses, the auxiliary must be considered *the* verb for purposes of placement, as in these examples:

Leur as-tu parlé? (interrogative inversion)
Nous les aurions vus. (preceded by object)
Il n'a rien dit. (surrounded by negatives)

When the verb is an affirmative imperative, the object follows it immediately.

Vas-y.
Achetez-le.
Parlons-en.
Téléphonez-leur.

In the negative imperative, the object is back before the verb.

N'y va pas.
Ne l'achetez pas.
N'en parlons plus.
Ne leur téléphonez jamais.

015 **ORDER OF OBJECT PRONOUNS**

As you know (if you didn't know, fake it), many verbs can take both direct and indirect objects. Take **give.** What you give is the direct object; the one to whom you give it is the indirect.

Je les (*direct*) donne aux enfants (*indirect*).
On leur (*indirect*) donne les jouets (*direct*).

You perceive the storm clouds gathering on the horizon, do you not? What if both objects are pronouns? They can't both come immediately before (or after) the verb. There must be some kind of pecking order.

Any rule about directs preceding indirects or vice versa becomes so cluttered with exceptions and special cases that it is useless or worse. The rule you are about to learn is entirely fortuitous. That it works is only a happy accident, but work it does, and without exception. There are three parts:

1. When both objects begin with the letter *L,* use them in alphabetical order.

>   Je les leur donne.
>   Donnez-les-leur.
>   Tu la lui prêtes.
>   Prête-la-lui.

   Note that position before or after the verb makes no difference. Alphabetical order is observed, reading from left to right.

2. When just one of the object pronouns begins with *L,* that one comes next to the verb.

>   Vous nous les envoyez.
>   Envoyez-les-nous.
>   Tu me la montres.
>   Montre-la-moi.

016   In final position, **me** and **te** become **moi** and **toi.** I'll explain that presently. Note the hyphens that always link a verb in the affirmative imperative with its object(s).

3. **Y** and **en** always come last (reading from left to right) in that order, **y** before **en.**

>   Tu leur en donneras.
>   Apportez-les-y.
>   Je n'y en ai pas mis.

Rule 3 sometimes conflicts with rule 2 (see the first of the above examples). When that happens, rule 3 always takes precedence.

Now here are some illustrations of the preceding rules. Each sentence appears twice: first with objects in italics and then with pronouns replacing them.

Il a donné plusieurs *claques* au *méchant garçon*.
Il lui en a donné plusieurs.

La balle a manqué *le président*.
La balle l'a manqué.

Ne prêtons pas *les livres à cet homme*.
Ne les lui prêtons pas.

Elle envoie *son fils en Europe*.
Elle l'y envoie.

Pouvez-vous parler *à votre père de vos projets?*
Pouvez-vous lui en parler?

Nous avons trouvé trois *sous dans la fontaine*.
Nous y en avons trouvé trois.

Il a vu *cette actrice sur la scène*.
Il l'y a vue.

Jetons *les miettes aux pauvres*.
Jetons-les-leur.

J'ai laissé *mon coeur à San Francisco*.
Je l'y ai laissé.

Thésée ne manquait guère *à Phèdre*.
Thésée ne lui manquait guère.

## 017   DISJUNCTIVE OR EMPHATIC PRONOUNS

What are disjunctives disjoined from? From the verb, that's what. Mostly they are objects of prepositions, so, coming at the ends of word groups, they carry the stress. **Me** and **te,** weak forms, cannot be stressed, which is why they become **moi** and **toi** in the affirmative imperative.

Tu feras ça pour moi?
Elle sort souvent avec lui.
Il réussira sans toi.

To emphasize the subject or object, double it with the appropriate emphatic pronoun.

> Moi, je déteste le caviar.
> Eux, ils ne se plaignent jamais.
> Tu ne l'attraperas plus, lui.

Another important use of the emphatics is in the expressions "Moi . . . aussi" and "Moi . . . non plus." French does not have exact equivalents of "So do we," "Neither can they," and so on. There are only "Nous aussi" and "Eux non plus," which are just like "We too" and "Neither do (will, can, have, etc.) they."

> You swam all day? So did she.
> Tu as nagé toute la journée? Elle aussi.

> We couldn't leave. Neither could they.
> Nous ne pouvions pas partir. Eux non plus.

When there are two or more subjects or objects, any of them that is a pronoun must be the emphatic. Again, this is usually doubled by the unstressed form.

> Lui et elle, ils vont se marier.
> Mon père et moi, nous ne nous entendons pas.
> Nous et eux, nous nous battrons.

Add the emphatic form to indicate strong contrast. "I'm talking to her" would normally be "Je lui parle," but in the sentence "I'm not talking to *you;* I'm talking to *her!*" we must use the emphatic to underscore the contrast: "Ce n'est pas à vous que je parle; c'est à elle!"

018  **IMPOSSIBLE COMBINATIONS**

Reflexives are never used together with indirect object pronouns. To avoid such gaffes, use the reflexive object and then a disjunctive.

> Je me suis présenté à toi il y a six ans.
> Il va s'adresser à nous.
> Elle se souvient d'eux.

OK. That was long and arduous, but now, having gotten through it, you feel an enormous sense of accomplishment, don't you? When you wake up, you will remember none of the hardship, but from now on, you will have no trouble with pronouns. You will, however, cluck like a chicken every time you hear the word "grammar." Wake up on the count of three. One . . . two . . .

# 3 ○ Relative Pronouns

019 **WHAT ARE THEY?**

The relative pronoun (RP) introduces a subordinate clause, specifically, a relative clause. If you know what a relative clause is and how it works, you may take three giant steps past the next paragraph.

020 A relative clause is part of a complex sentence, in which there are a main clause and one or more subordinate clauses. In the following examples, the relative clauses are in italics:

1. Give me some men *who are stout-hearted men.*
2. The hand *that rocks the cradle* rules the world.
3. It followed her to school one day, *which was against the rule.*

Note that the relative clauses are adjectival. They inform us about part (examples 1 and 2) or all (example 3) of the main clause. Note also that they may sometimes come between parts of the main clause, as in example 2, in which the main clause is "The hand rules the world." The relative clause "that rocks the cradle" tells us more about the hand, helps us identify it. Finally, relative clauses cannot stand by themselves as sentences.

021 **FORMS OF THE FRENCH RP**

Two factors determine the form of the RP: the antecedent, that is, the person or thing the RP represents, and the function of the RP

**17**

*in its own clause.* Consider RPs as two-faced, looking in two directions—back to the antecedent and ahead to the function. The illustrations may not be at all helpful, but we have to dress up the page.

The RPs are **qui, que, dont, où, lequel** (and its variants), and **quoi.** I was sorely tempted to omit that last one, which tends to muddy otherwise limpid waters, but someone would be sure to blow the whistle.

Here are the factors that determine which one is used:

1. the antecedent, which is either a person or a nonperson;
2. the function: in its own clause, the RP may be subject, direct object, or indirect object (object of a preposition).

Monsieur RP (Morp) is unhappy because there seem to be so many things to consider. Let us hasten to his aid.

022   **RP AS SUBJECT**

If the antecedent is a person and the function is subject then the RP is **qui.**

(In all the following examples, the RP and its antecedent are underscored. The relative clause is italicized.)

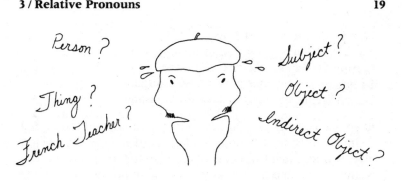

Où est le <u>garçon</u> *qui soigne les brebis?*
Il y avait une vieille <u>femme</u> *qui habitait un soulier.*
J. Sprat, *qui ne mangeait pas de graisse,* était mince.
Je connais un <u>homme</u> *qui ne sait pas lire.*
C'est le pauvre <u>Humpty</u> *qui est tombé.*

If the antecedent is a nonperson and the function is subject then the RP is **qui.**

Il vint une <u>araignée</u> *qui s'assit à côté d'elle.*
C'est la <u>curiosité</u> *qui a tué le chat.*
<u>Chien</u> *qui aboie* ne mord jamais.
L'<u>auto</u>, *qui n'a pas de bougies,* ne marche pas.
Voici le <u>pistolet</u> *qui prouve ses accusations.*

023  **RP AS DIRECT OBJECT**

If the antecedent is a person and the function is direct object then the RP is **que.**

Voilà l'<u>homme</u> *que vous avez nommé.*
Il y a des <u>enfants</u> *que je ne peux pas supporter.*
La <u>voisine</u> *que tu connaissais* a déménagé.
Le <u>docteur</u> *que nous avions appelé* n'a pas pu venir.
Comment s'appelle la <u>fille</u> *qu'il a sortie hier soir?*

If the antecedent is a nonperson and the function is direct object then the RP is **que.**

La robe *qu'elle porte* est jolie.
J'ai trouvé l'argent *que vous aviez caché.*
C'est le fleuve *que Washington traversa.*
La plume *que ma tante avait achetée* a disparu.
La conférence *que nous écoutons* est amusante.

And so, dear reader, as you have surely noticed, perhaps even a trifle impatiently, the RP subject is always **qui** and the direct object is always **que.** I divided them according to the humanity or "un-humanity" of antecedent to give you a little practice in spotting antecedents. This becomes crucial when we deal with indirect objects.

Please remember that it is always safe to put the relative clause immediately after its antecedent (and modifiers, if any). Departure from this order is perilous.

024   **RP AS NONHUMAN INDIRECT OBJECT**

Now you must be introduced to the Lequel family: Papa Lequel, Maman Laquelle, all the little Lesquels, and their sisters, the Lesquelles.

Here's how it works. (Keep on some mental back burner that there are exceptions to what I am about to tell you, but be secure in the knowledge that these rules will cover all but an insignificant number of cases.)

1. **Lequel** is made up of the definite article plus **quel,** both of which agree with the antecedent in gender and number.

2. Except for the exceptions (I warned you), the antecedent of **lequel** is nonhuman.

3. **Lequel** (etc.) is nearly always the object of a preposition, so we have "pour lequel," "avec laquelle," "sans lesquelles," etc.

4. Combinations of **à** and **de** with the first part of this RP result, as you would expect, in the following:

   à + lequel = auquel, à + lesquels = auxquels,
   à + lesquelles = auxquelles.

la chose

de laquelle
pour laquelle
à laquelle
etc.

de + lequel = duquel, de + lesquels = desquels,
de + lesquelles = desquelles.

Note the appearance of the two-faced gentleman again, this time illustrating the use of a member of the **lequel** family.

Here are some further examples:

Voilà la table sous laquelle le fugitif s'était caché.
Où est le cheval sur lequel elle fut montée hier?
Les maisons vers lesquelles vous vous dirigez sont encore loin.
Les fleurs auxquelles tu penses sont fanées.
Ce sont des choses sans lesquelles elle échouerait.

025 **HUMAN INDIRECT OBJECTS**

When the antecedent is human and the function is object of a preposition then the RP is **qui.**

Je déteste l'homme pour qui je travaille.
Les jeunes filles avec qui elle joue crient trop.
C'est une amie sans qui elle échouerait.

NOTE: Although English sentences and clauses regularly violate the old rule about not ending with a preposition ("I hate the man I work *for.*" "The girls she plays *with* are too noisy."), only in very familiar French are prepositions ever final.

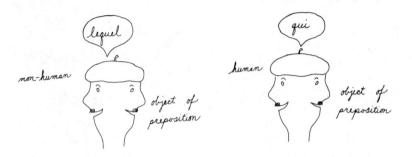

Note how Morp says it.

## ALTERNATIVES: DONT AND OU

Now for a bit of overlapping, of redundancy.

026 First of all: **dont.** That may sound like good advice, but it isn't intended that way. We aren't here to establish moral imperatives. The French RP **dont** is our target. **Dont** is an alternative to **de qui** and to **duquel** (etc.). In other words, **dont** may be used instead of **de** plus any other RP. That's not a strong enough statement. The fact is that **dont** is used more frequently than any of the other RPs that might serve the same purpose. It is preferable to **de qui, duquel,** etc.

> Les hommes dont il a peur sont sortis.
> Voici les animaux dont j'ai rêvé.
> C'est une maison dont les portes sont toujours fermées.
> Il cherche le cor dont Roland a sonné.
> Je connais une femme dont le fils habite en Chine.

One more thing: **dont** must always come immediately after its antecedent (and modifiers, if any) and must be followed immediately by the subject of the subordinate clause.

> Elle cache le gâteau (*antecedent*) dont il (*subject*) a envie.
> C'est un monsieur (*antecedent*) dont je (*subject*) connais le père.

Où est le cheval de bois (*antecedent with modifier*) dont l'enfant (*subject*) a parlé?

Try translating the second of those into English and see what happens to the word order.

027   And then there's **où**. As RP, **où** may be used instead of the **lequel** family when the antecedent is a place. Its central meaning is "where." **Où** never stands for a person.

Ouvrons le placard où il se cache.
C'est un pays où j'aimerais vivre.
N'aimes-tu pas l'école où tu vas tous les jours?
La salle où j'étudie est toujours vide.

## A FEW STRAY ITEMS

028   The French RP must have a one-word antecedent. We must be able to point to a word in the main clause and exclaim, triumphantly, "Aha! Eureka! That word is the antecedent!" So what happens when the RP stands for the whole main clause, as in "It followed her to school one day, which was against the rule"? What happens is that **ce** is introduced to serve as the grammatical antecedent. It tells us that the real antecedent is the whole clause.

Il a avalé le poisson rouge, ce qui nous a fait rire.
Vous avez mangé mon croissant, ce qui m'ennuie.
Il ment, ce que nous condamnons.
Le semestre se termine, ce dont les étudiants se réjouissent.

Obviously, the whole main clause must be understood as the real antecedent in all those sentences. Look at the first. Without **ce,** we'd be obliged to take "poisson" as the antecedent, and the statement would be silly (sillier?)

029   I can't put **quoi** off any longer. It sometimes serves as RP, always as a nonperson, and always as object of a preposition. You can get along nicely without ever using it actively (except as an interrogative), but do recognize it. It is the only exception to the rule about definite one-word antecedents.

Il sait de quoi il parle.

Elle n'a pas de quoi acheter ce vison.

J'ai hurlé, sans quoi ils ne m'auraient jamais remarqué.

030   In English, the RP is often omitted and understood:

The bus (that) he took goes the wrong way.

In French, the RP is never omitted.

This is my last chance to make faces at you. The following are Morp's-eye views of the RP.

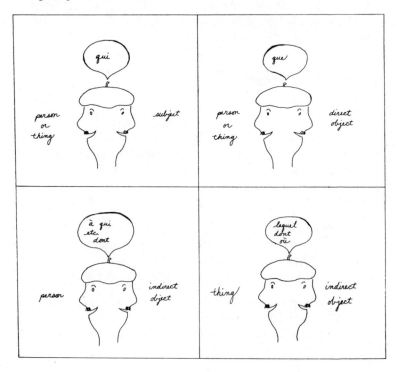

# 4 ○ Passé Composé and Imperfect

Before we start, please accept that there is no exact equivalent for either of these tenses in English. Accepted? Good! Now we can start.

## 031 FRENCH PASSE COMPOSE AND ENGLISH PRESENT PERFECT

Confusion of these tenses, which look, smell, feel, and taste alike, is understandable, but:

The English present perfect *must* bring us up to the present. It is a statement of what *has happened* so far, not of what *did happen* at some time unconnected with the present.

The left column below is for the past *only*. On the right are time frames that may include past events but that do comprise the present:

| | |
|---|---|
| 1862 | This year |
| Yesterday | Today |
| The nineteenth century | The twentieth century |

The time indicated on the right may be a nanosecond, an hour, or an eon. Length of time doesn't matter. The important thing is that it must still be going on. Only when that is true may the English present perfect be used.

| | |
|---|---|
| In 1870, my grandfather didn't travel. | This year, I have already visited eight foreign countries. |
| Yesterday we met once. | Today we have met several times. |

Like the present perfect, the French passé composé can bring us up to the present, but it can also refer to something entirely in the past. Here are the last two examples in French:

| | |
|---|---|
| En 1870 mon grand-père n'a pas voyagé. | Cette année-ci, j'ai déjà visité huit pays étrangers. |
| Hier, nous nous sommes rencontrés une fois. | Aujourd'hui, nous nous sommes rencontrés plusieurs fois. |

Perhaps you have noticed this: a common mistake made by a Frenchman whose English is less than perfect is to say things like "We have had a good time at the party last night." That kind of thing happens because the passé composé can refer to the unconnected past and the present perfect cannot.

The following sentences further illustrate the difference:

| *English:* | *French:* |
|---|---|
| They went out yesterday. | Elles sont sorties hier. |
| They have gone out today. | Elles sont sorties aujourd'hui. |

"They have gone out yesterday" is not a possible English sentence.

| *English:* | *French:* |
|---|---|
| We read it last week. | Nous l'avons lu la semaine dernière. |
| We have read it tonight. | Nous l'avons lu ce soir. |

"We have read it last week" is not a possible English sentence.

I think I may be flogging a dead horse. (What a revolting figure of speech!) Let's move on.

032  **THE PASSE SIMPLE**

The passé simple is not used in conversation or in informal writing. We could call it the passé composé in formal dress, only it doesn't do everything the passé composé does. It is limited to the remote past; it cannot make contact with the present.

All the following sentences can use either tense. The determining factor is the formality or informality of the discourse.

Jefferson a écrit (écrivit) la déclaration.
C. C. a traversé (traversa) l'océan en 1492.
Le général a été (fut) blessé à l'épaule.
Le roi est mort (mourut) en 1793.

But these, which do show connections to the present moment, must be in the passé composé:

Jusqu'ici, elle ne m'a pas remarqué.
Je n'ai pas déjeuné aujourd'hui.
L'herbe a déjà assez poussé.
De ma vie je n'ai pas vu de vache pourpre.
Où est-ce que tout notre argent a disparu cette année?

033 **PASSE COMPOSE OR IMPERFECT**

A partial layout of tenses with the past on the left and, on the right, those that touch the present, might look like this:

| passé composé | passé composé |
| passé simple | |
| imperfect | |
| English past | English present perfect |

On the right, where we find both the passé composé and the English present perfect, there's nothing to ruffle our serenity. Remember that the passé composé can start in the remote or unconnected past (last May) and bring us up to the present (this month).

On the left, leaving out the passé simple, which, remember, is only a more formal passé composé (but limited to remote past), we are left with both passé composé and imperfect *to cover the same time span as the English simple past.* Aye, there's the rub! They both refer to the same time span. So why bother with two of them? What's the difference? Now we get to the scintillating part of my exposition (there's at least one in each chapter).

These two tenses indicate different *views* of an event. The imperfect stresses that it had amplitude, that it took time, that it was a process. The passé composé makes a tighter package. It refers to an event as a discrete thing, perhaps one in a series. It does not stress the fact that the event happened over time.

Of course, any event can be viewed as a moment or as a succession of moments. Seen from most angles, for instance, this row of dots— . . . . . . . . . .—looks like a row of dots. But imagine yourself at one end, looking at it with one eye closed (or, if you prefer, with one eye open). You would see just one dot. The row is like the imperfect, and the single dot is like the passé composé. The event doesn't change; the point of view changes.

I know you'd rather have a few solid, memorizable, exceptionless rules than all this discussion, but just between you and me, that isn't the way language works. It wasn't built like a bridge, according to clear, logical precepts; it just grew.

Nevertheless, there are a few rules of thumb for you to sink your teeth into. (Be careful of those thumbs!) In almost every case, they are simple expressions of the differences outlined above. Here they are:

034   1. Whenever English uses, or could use, the progressive form, "was (or were) ——ing," the French tense is the imperfect.

| | |
|---|---|
| You were saying . . . | Vous disiez . . . |
| We were eating. | Nous mangions. |
| I was resting. | Je me reposais. |

2. Whenever English uses, or could use, the words **used to** or **would** (in the sense of "used to"), the French tense is the imperfect.

| | |
|---|---|
| She used to smile often. | Elle souriait souvent. |
| We used to take walks. | Nous nous promenions. |
| They would cry at funerals. | Ils pleuraient aux funérailles. |

Be sure not to confuse the **would** that means "used to" and the conditional **would.** The former is the one we're concerned with here. It always implies repetition or duration in the past. This short paragraph can serve as an example:

> Lorsque Papa entrait dans notre chambre, nous faisions semblant d'étudier. Plus tard, il nous a dit qu'il toussait toujours pour nous avertir avant d'ouvrir la porte.

> When Papa came (would come, used to come) into our room, we pretended (would pretend, used to pretend) to be studying. Later, he told us that he always coughed (would cough, used to cough) to warn us before opening the door.

I'll deal with the conditional **would** soon.

There are no exceptions to the rules about "was (were) ——ing" and "used to (would) ——." But where English has only a simple past, you must exercise your judgment. The sentence "We went to the theatre" could call for a passé composé or an imperfect. Context tells us which. It doesn't always tell us in a loud, clear voice. On the contrary, it often whispers so faintly that even the keen ears of the Frenchman may strain to get the message. In other words, a few cases straddle the line so well that the only thing for us poor outlanders to do is toss a centime. Fortunately, the great majority of cases are quite clear.

Here are a couple of examples of context speaking audibly:

> To celebrate my last birthday, *we went to the theatre* and then to a good restaurant. (Use passé composé. Context does not stress duration or suggest repetition.) Pour fêter mon dernier anniversaire, *nous sommes allés au théâtre* et puis à un bon restaurant.

> At that time, *we went to the theatre* every week. (Use imperfect. The idea is clearly one of repetition over a period of time.) A cette époque-là, *nous allions au théâtre* toutes les semaines.

Other clues: States of being are *more likely* to be in the imperfect than in the passé composé. They are *usually* seen as being continuous. Please take careful note of the italicized words in those sentences. Probability is what you get, statistical preponderance.

What you don't get is absolute certainty. In some contexts, for instance, all of the examples below could be in the passé composé. That could happen rather easily in the first two. It would be almost but not quite impossible in the third.

> Le ciel était bleu.
> La radio ne marchait pas.
> Il avait une jambe de bois.

When there is a background against which an event takes place, the background is in the imperfect and the event in the passé composé:

> Il arrosait son jardin quand tu l'as salué.
> Les nuages roulaient. Soudain, nous avons vu le premier éclair.

Of course the two things indicated can both be continuous:

> Tu jouais du piano pendant que je lisais.
> Vous étudiiez beaucoup. Lui, il allait à des parties.
> Phèdre aimait Hippolyte, mais il s'intéressait à une autre.

These are like protracted parallel lines.

When the two ends of a time period are given in the sentence, the verb is *more likely than not* (how's that for a weasel phrase?) to be in the passé composé. Please remember, though, that any time "used to ———" or "was (were) ——ing" would fit, the verb is in the imperfect.

> Entre quatre heures et six heures elle a dormi.

(But, of course, if the context is anything like, "She used to sleep between four and six, during those boring lectures," or "She was sleeping between four and six while the burglar was emptying the house," use imperfect.)

035    Another thing: You are familiar with sentences having an **if** clause expressing a condition contrary to fact and a result clause in the conditional. (This is the conditional **would** I promised we'd get to.) Some English examples are:

> If wishes were horses (they aren't), then beggars would ride.

If I had a hammer (I haven't), I'd swing it in the morning.
I wouldn't marry you if you were the last man on earth (you
aren't).

In French, the **if** clause of such sentences is in the imperfect.

Si vous aviez le temps, je vous raconterais l'histoire de ma vie.
Si la lettre arrivait, nous la lirions.
S'il ne faisait jamais froid, est-ce que la chair des poules serait
lisse?

036  Context, as I've been suggesting, is crucial. The only way ade-
quately to illustrate the use of tenses is in a continuous narrative.
Well, what a coincidence. Here comes one now!

Ce matin-là, je me *suis levé* à six heures. Je me *lavais* les dents
quand le tremblement de terre nous *a frappés*. Entre 1950 et
1970 il y *a eu* plusieurs tremblements de terre à Paris. La première
fois, j'*habitais* chez mon oncle. Au premier choc, ma tante *a
ouvert* ma porte. Elle *avait* très peur. Elle *pleurait* en se rongeant
les ongles.

Soudain, l'autre moitié de la maison *est tombée* dans un énorme
trou. Mon oncle *lisait* son journal dans le salon. Pendant qu'il
*disparaissait* dans le gouffre, il *a tourné* une dernière page.

*Explanation:*

*suis levé*  The narrator is referring to a particular morning, not
   to his general practice.
*lavais*  The procedure must be seen as having duration, since it
   is about to be interrupted by an event.
*a frappés*  This is a single event. The earthquake took time, of
   course, but we are considering the moment of its onset.
*a eu*  The time limits are marked, and there is no contraindication.
*habitais*  This is a continuing condition. The English might be
   "was living."
*a ouvert*  This is viewed as a moment, without duration.
*avait*  A continuing state.
*pleurait*  Seen as having duration: "was crying."
*est tombée*  A momentary event.

*lisait*   Continuous. English might be "was reading."
*disparaissait*   It looks like a moment, but here it serves as background for another event.
*a tourné*   The event that occurs against that background.

On the assumption that that was helpful, here's another equally profound little story:

Il *pleuvait* depuis cinq jours, et les enfants *commençaient* à m'agacer. Enfin, lundi, je les *ai mis* dans un placard. Entre six heures et minuit ils *ont hurlé*. Ma femme *a dit* qu'il n'y *avait* pas assez d'air là-dedans pour les sept petits. Cela m'*a énervé* davantage. Je l'y *ai enfermée* avec eux. Après, tout *a été* calme.

Un mois plus tard, un agent *a frappé* à ma porte. Il *voulait* savoir pourquoi mes enfants n'*allaient* plus à l'école. Alors j'*ai ouvert* le placard et je les lui *ai montrés*.

Si vous m'*envoyiez* une scie, je pourrais sortir de cette cellule.

*Explanation:*

*pleuvait*   Continuity stressed. "It had been raining. . . ."
*commençaient*   This is not a single moment but a string of moments. You might say "were beginning."
*ai mis*   We are not at all concerned with duration of this act.
*ont hurlé*   Two ends marked. No contraindication.
*a dit*   A single event. We have no interest in its duration.
*avait*   A continuing state.
*a énervé*   The single result of a single act.
*ai enfermée*   No concern with duration. One in a series of events.
*a été*   The result of an act. Things *became* calm.
*a frappé*   Another in the series of events. No interest in duration.
*voulait*   A continuing state of mind.
*allaient*   A daily, repeated practice.
*ai ouvert*   Another in the series of events.
*ai montrés*   Ditto.
*envoyiez*   A condition, not a fact. The **if** clause followed by a conditional.

# 5 ○ Agreement of Participles

Unlike the Treaty of Paris and the Geneva Convention, the Agreement of Participles was never signed by a diplomat, but it is still in force.

### 037 PRECEDING DIRECT OBJECTS

Let's start with something beautifully simple: The past participle always agrees in gender and number with a preceding direct object (PDO). That's all there is to it. The one small exception I can think of involves causative **faire.** It is treated at 118.

> Les voleurs? Nous ne les avons pas vus. (*Vus* agrees with the PDO *les,* which stands for the masculine plural *voleurs.*)

> Madame, je vous aurais suivie. (*Suivie* agrees with the PDO *vous,* which stands for the feminine singular *Madame.*)

> Henri, on t'aura chassé. (*Chassé* agrees with the PDO *t',* which stands for the masculine singular *Henri.*)

> Les voitures qu'ils avaient réparées étaient en panne. (*Réparées* agrees with the PDO *qu',* which stands for the feminine plural *voitures.*)

(For more on direct objects, see 009 and 046.)

### 038 PASSIVE

As indicated in another, equally memorable chapter the participle always agrees with the subject of a passive (see 064). This is neither a contradiction nor a complication. The passive in French can be formed only when the verb is transitive, so that the subject is also the PDO, the *direct* recipient of the action.

> Elle a été découverte en 1843. (*Elle*, the subject, is also the direct object of *découvrir*.)
>
> Nous serons surveillés par le gardien. (*Nous*, the subject, is also the direct object of *surveiller*.)
>
> Mon frère aurait été libéré. (*Frère*, the subject, is also the direct object of *libérer*.)

If any of this is troublesome, I modestly suggest you look at chapter 7, where it is set forth with uncommon lucidity and thoroughness.

039 **AGREEMENT IN REFLEXIVES** (See also chapter 6.)

This may appear to be a contradiction to the rule about PDOs, but it conforms perfectly. Here's the source of the confusion. Usually the reflexive pronoun *is* a PDO. By definition, the reflexive object is the same person as the subject. Ergo, the participle often is of the same gender and number as the subject too, as in

> Elle s'est assise.

Such agreement with the subject is, however, coincidental. Look at what happens when there is no PDO:

> Elle s'est chanté une chanson.

The thing she sang is a song. She sang it *to* herself. "Chanson" is the direct object, and it comes *after* the verb. There is no PDO and no agreement. The preceding object is indirect.

> Les garçons se sont lavé les mains. (No PDO)
> Les garçons se sont baignés. (PDO)
>
> Elle s'est payé une nouvelle voiture. (No PDO)
> Voilà la nouvelle voiture qu'elle s'est payée. (PDO)
>
> Je me suis brossé les dents. (No PDO)
> Je me les suis brossées. (PDO)

040   **ETRE VERBS**

Here are some old friends, the **être** verbs. In case you have forgotten their names, permit me to reintroduce you. They are **aller,
arriver, descendre, entrer, monter, mourir, naître, partir,
rentrer, rester, retourner, sortir, tomber,** and **venir.** These
verbs use **être,** not **avoir,** as the auxiliary in compound tenses.

> Je suis descendu.
> Tu n'étais pas encore retourné.
> Notre ami sera-t-il mort?

The **être** verbs are sometimes called "intransitive verbs of motion."
That isn't even a nice try. Many intransitive verbs of motion don't
belong to the group—**marcher** and **plonger,** for example. And
how, by that definition, does **mourir** fit? Transmigration of souls?

041   A mnemonic maneuver that works is to call them the "Mrs. Vandertramp" (MrsV) verbs. In that title and name are all their initial
letters.

Also, any of the MrsV verbs with a prefix is still a member of the
group. For instance, **convenir, contrevenir, devenir, inter-
venir, redevenir, revenir,** and **survenir,** all **venir** with different
prefixes, are all **être** verbs. Inclusion of all such possibilities individually would make the list unmanageably long.

042   **DISTINCTION OF ETRE VERBS FROM REFLEXIVES**
(See also chapter 6.)

No matter how you do it, it is essential that you memorize the
MrsV verbs as a separate set. When they are in compound tenses,
the participle agrees with the subject. They must be learned separately and kept distinct from the reflexives, which are also conjugated with **être** in compound tenses. In the case of the reflexives,
however (yes, this is a repetition of 039—it seemed appropriate),
the subject does *not* affect the participle. They often agree, but only
coincidentally, and that can't serve as the basis for any kind of
rule. Reflexive participles are affected only by PDOs.

> Elle est partie. (Participle agrees with subject of **être** verb.)

Elle s'est lavée. (Participle appears to agree with subject.)
*but*
Elle s'est lavé les mains. (No PDO, no **être** verb, no agreement.)
Nous étions tombés. (Participle agrees with subject of **être** verb.)
Nous nous étions maquillées. (Participle appears to agree with subject.)
*but*
Nous nous étions maquillé les yeux. (No PDO, no **être** verb, no agreement.)

043   It just occurred to me that in order to understand this fully, you really should be sure of the difference between transitive and intransitive verbs. If you are insulted by the suggestion that you may be shaky on that point (which is also touched on in paragraphs 009 and 010), please skip the rest of 043.

It isn't very complicated. The transitive verb has a direct object, and the intransitive has an indirect or none at all.

*Transitive:*              *Intransitive:*
Tu tues ton tuteur.        Raymond répond.

Note that many verbs can be used either way.

*Transitive:*              *Intransitive:*
Elle parle français.       Elle parle à son père.
Je pense "Zut alors!"      Je pense profondément.
Les jeunes gens jouent un  Les jeunes gens jouent.
  quatuor de Brahms.

044   **TRANSITIVE USE OF ETRE VERBS**

Meanwhile, back at Mrs. Vandertramp's ranch, there's just one more dogie to be branded. The **être** verbs are mostly intransitive, but a few of them can be used transitively: **descendre, monter, retourner,** and **sortir.**

*Intransitive:*            *Transitive:*
Les avions descendent.     Ils descendent l'escalier.
Nous montons ensemble.     Nous montons les valises.
Elle retourne fatiguée.    Elle retourne le livre.

Ma femme sort le soir.          Ma femme sort son mouchoir.

When these verbs are used transitively, their compound tenses are formed with **avoir** and the participle does not agree with the subject. As examples, let's take the same four.

*Intransitive:*                           *Transitive:*
Les avions sont descendus.            Ils ont descendu l'échelle.
Nous étions montés ensemble.          Nous avions monté les valises.
Elle serait retournée fatiguée.       Elle aurait retourné les livres.
Ma femme est sortie ce soir.          Ma femme aura sorti son
                                      mouchoir.

When they are used transitively, those verbs follow the PDO rule. Here are the last four sentences with pronouns replacing the noun objects.

> Ils l'ont descendue.
> Nous les avions montées.
> Elle les aurait retournés.
> Ma femme l'aura sorti.

And while we're in the neighborhood, we may as well at least glance at the fact that **monter,** used transitively, can be "go" up (a stairway) or "take" up (the groceries). Same story, in reverse, for **descendre.**

045 **SUMMARY OF RULES FOR AGREEMENT**

Now here's what you put under your pillow at night. The past participle agrees with just three things:

1. the subject of an **être** verb;
2. the subject of a passive;
3. a preceding direct object.

**OBJECTS**

046 **Direct**

In most cases, verbs that are transitive in English are also transitive in French, so your wild guesses will usually be right. There are some notable exceptions, which deserve to be learned.

**Approuver, attendre, chercher, écouter,** and **regarder** all take direct objects.

Another way of saying that is: the French don't wait *for*, listen *to*, approve *of*, look *at*, or look *for* something. On attend, approuve, cherche, écoute, ou regarde quelque chose ou quelqu'un.

047 **Indirect**

Again, these are usually like English, but there are some important differences: **obéir, plaire,** and **téléphoner** come to mind. In French, you can't obey, please, or telephone anyone. On obéit *à* quelqu'un, on plaît *à* quelqu'un, on téléphone *à* quelqu'un.

048 **LAST LOOSE END**

**En** sometimes looks like a PDO, and evidently some grammarians are fooled into believing that it *can* be one. We do not share their naïveté. In any case, the participle never agrees with **en** or **y.**

049 Finally, here are some illustrations for you to contemplate serenely. Where there is agreement of participle, the reason is given at the end.

Bizarre! Il aimait une femme qui était morte il y avait des siècles.
   (**Etre** verb)
Si j'avais su qu'elles venaient, je les aurais attendues. (PDO)
Les éléphants n'ont pas étonné les enfants. Ils en avaient vu en
   Inde.
On avait oublié de fermer le gaz. Heureusement, elle s'est rév-
   eillée. (PDO)
Ill fallait que son mari aille au bureau. Elle l'a donc réveillé.
   (PDO)
Le club a besoin de membres. Nous serons acceptés. (Passive)
Dépêchons-nous! Maman sera arrivée à la gare. (**Etre** verb)
Elle ne savait pas l'histoire. Ne lui avais-tu pas téléphoné?
Les dames que vous avez insultées vont porter plainte. (PDO)

And now, as this chapter strolls hand in hand into the brilliant sunset, we hear exotic birds (parrots?) singing, ''The past participle agrees with just three things:

1. the subject of an **être** verb;
2. the subject of a passive;
3. a preceding direct object.''

# 6 ○ Reflexives

**WHAT ARE THEY?**

First, understand that the name "reflexive verb" is misleading. There are very few French verbs that are always reflexive. Others may or may not be *used* reflexively.

Think of the etymological meaning of the word. **Re** is "back" or "again" and **flex** is "bend." A verb used reflexively denotes an action performed by the subject *on the subject,* a turning back or boomerang effect.

Je me promène *means literally*
I promenade myself *so we translate it as*
I take a walk (or a turn, à bicyclette, en auto, etc.).

Elle se couche *means literally*
She lays herself down *so we translate it as*
She goes to bed.

Il se parle *means literally*
He talks to himself *so we translate it as*
He talks to himself.

But these verbs, like nearly all the so-called reflexives, can also be used nonreflexively; that is, the subject acts not on himself but on someone or something else.

Le soir je promène le chien.

Elle couche le bébé à sept heures.
Il parle à la classe.

## 051 PRONOMINAL VERBS

All the reflexive verbs belong to the group the French call "verbes pronominaux." The name means simply that the verb carries its own object pronoun, the same in person and number as the subject. But not all verbes pronominaux (let's call them VEEPS) are reflexive, as we'll soon see, so let's get used to the broader term.

## 052 VEEP OBJECTS

In textbook vocabulary lists, verbs used pronominally are usually given as **se** + infinitive: "se lever," "s'appeler," etc. Some students (I'll name no names. You know who you are!), seeing this, assume that **se** is the only pronoun to be used with an infinitive VEEP. Not so! You know the whole batch: **me, te, se, nous, vous, se.** Use the appropriate one, the one that corresponds to the subject. The **se** + infinitive found in vocabulary lists simply means that the verb has a pronominal use. Take the English pronoun **oneself.** "To know oneself," "se connaître," is an infinitive as it might appear in a vocabulary list. "One needs to know oneself" ("On a besoin de se connaître") is a reasonable sentence, but "I need to know oneself" is nonsense. Its French equivalent would be equally meaningless.

If you have long held these truths to be self-evident, please forgive my including them here. Believe me; some people need the reminder.

Here are some examples of infinitive VEEPS with the proper pronouns:

As-tu envie de *te* moucher?
Je veux *me* baigner dans la mer.
Elle n'a pas le courage de *s'*habiller tout en pourpre.
Nous devons *nous* coucher avant onze heures.
Ils refusent de *se* raser le samedi.

**Parts of the Self**

Here's a distinction that may prove useful: you can do things *to* or *with* parts of your body. The French pattern changes accordingly.

First *to*. The part referred to in these instances is completely passive. It is acted upon, not active. Use VEEP object and, when necessary, specify the part.

Tu devrais te brosser les dents.
Le pécheur se battait la poitrine.
Elle s'est lavé la tête.
Ne vous rongez pas les ongles.

Note that all of those would work, grammatically, without specification of the part. It would simply be understood that the whole body was the object. In that case the first example, depending on the firmness of the brush, could suggest something painful. On the other hand, there's no need to specify "les cheveux" after "Elle se peigne." What else would she comb?

Now *with*. The part named plays an active role. In such cases, the verb is not pronominal, nor is there a possessive, as there is in English.

Je lève la main.
Il tire la langue.
Le chien baisse les oreilles.
Elle avance lentement le pied.
Pourquoi fronces-tu le sourcils?

The natural assumption is that I raise my own hand, that he sticks out his own tongue, etc. Of course context *could* change things.

L'étudiant en médecine lève la main de son cadavre.

WARNING: The surgeon-general has determined that this *to–with* distinction doesn't always work. For instance, in the sentence "L'Esquimau se frotte les mains," he does something both *to* and *with* them. Still, I think it works often enough to be helpful.

053   **ACTION VS. STATE**

Think about the sentence "She sits in an armchair." Does it refer to the act of sitting down or to the state of "seatedness"? In English, depending on the context, it could be either.

She arrives out of breath and sits in an armchair. (*action*)
She sits in an armchair all day waiting for him. (*state*)

In French, the action is expressed one way, with a VEEP, and the resultant state in another way, with an adjective (often the participle of the verb). "To sit", the action, is "s'asseoir." "He sits" = "Il s'assied." The state, with no movement suggested, is expressed in this case with the participle used as an adjective. "He sits" = "Il est assis."

This whole brouhaha regards only about a half dozen verbs and their resultant states.

se lever (the act of standing)
être debout (the state of standing)

s'asseoir (the act of sitting)
être assis (the state of sitting)

se coucher (the act of lying down)
être couché (the state of lying down)

You get the message. Among other pairs that work the same way are

s'accouder–être accoudé
s'adosser–être adossé
s'allonger–être allongé
se pencher–être penché

The first three, the ones set apart, are used particularly often. They deserve this attention.

054 **COMPOUND TENSES**

All VEEPS are conjugated with **être** in compound tenses.

Il s'est habillé.
Je me serais tu.
Tu t'étais endormi.

But when the same verbs are used as other than VEEPS, they are conjugated with **avoir.**

Il a habillé son petit fils.
J'aurais tu la vérité.
La musique t'avait endormi.

055  The past participle of a VEEP in a compound tense agrees in gender
and number with a PDO, and *only* with a PDO (see 037). Frequently, but by no means always, the PDO of a VEEP is the same
person as the subject. This has caused a few of my more benighted
colleagues to state that the participle of a VEEP agrees with its
subject. I hereby disinherit them.

Elle s'est lavée.
*but*
Elle s'est lavé les mains.

(For greater clarification, see chapter 5, particularly 039, 042,
and 043.)


## OTHER USES OF VEEPS

Up to this point we've been dealing with the reflexive, which is
the most common application of the VEEP, but the others are important too. They are: *reciprocal, passive,* and *idiomatic.*

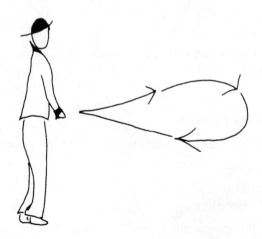

056 **Reciprocal**

In their plural forms, and with the same object pronouns as reflexives, Veeps may indicate reciprocal action. The reflexive in English uses words like **himself, itself, ourselves.** The key words for the reciprocal are **each other.**

If the first drawing represents the reflexive, then the second is the reciprocal.

The subjects do something not to themselves but to each other. (They don't even have to be consenting adults.)

"Elle se déteste," being singular, is clearly reflexive, but how about "Elles se détestent"? Do they hate themselves or each other? It could be either. Context makes it clear.

Marie a essayé d'empoisonner Jeanne, et Jeanne a envoyé une bombe à Marie. Elles se détestent.

*or*

Toutes les femmes qui souffrent de cette psychose ont le même problème: elles se détestent.

If you had much trouble deciding which of those sentences is

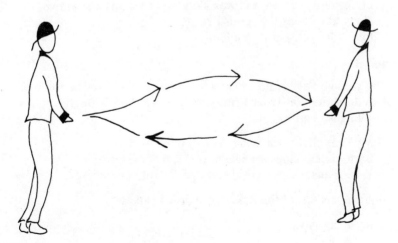

reflexive and which reciprocal, drop French immediately. Major in remedial macramé.

057   A transitive reciprocal VEEP may be followed by "l'un(e) l'autre" or by its plural, "les un(e)s les autres." This formula stresses that the action goes both ways and so makes it certain that the statement or question will be understood as reciprocal, not reflexive.

Elle et sa grand'mère s'aiment l'une l'autre.
Les éléphants et les souris se craignent les uns les autres.
Le médecin et le malade s'aident l'un l'autre.
Les Grecs et les Troyens se sont attaqués les uns les autres.
La mère et sa fille se comprennent l'une l'autre.

True confession: I have thought long, hard, and ineffectively about intransitive verbs using that formula, and about its use with verbs that are not pronominal. Every tentative generalization had so many exceptions, the complications were so convoluted, that I don't think it would be a good idea to try including them. Just be informed that sometimes there's a preposition and that it occupies the place indicated in these examples:

Elle et sa grand'mère se parlent l'une à l'autre.
Les éléphants et les souris se méfient les uns des autres.
Les généraux et lex amiraux s'obéissent les uns aux autres.
Nous travaillons l'un pour l'autre.
Elle et lui pensent l'un à l'autre.

058   **Passive**

The passive VEEP is no cinch to pin down either. Maybe the best way to show you what I mean by passive VEEP is to give you a few English equivalents:

My dear chap, that *is not done* in polite society.
Barfo potato chips *are sold* at fine stores everywhere.
Your reluctance to wrestle an ape *is* easily *understood*.

French versions of the italicized words would be:

ne se fait pas
se vendent

se comprend

They are passive VEEPS.

GROUND RULES: The subject of a passive VEEP is a nonperson. The action is not something done once by a particular person or group; it is more general. The object, like those of all passives in French, is direct.

In just about all cases, an alternative expression meaning very much the same could be formed with **on** as subject. (See 067.)

Les montagnes se voient le matin.
On voit les montagnes le matin.

De telles choses se disent entre amis.
On dit de telles choses entre amis.

Les bureaux s'ouvrent à huit heures précises.
On ouvre les bureaux à huit heures précises.

La nouvelle se raconte partout.
On raconte la nouvelle partout.

Ca se fait dans les grandes villes.
On fait ça dans les grandes villes.

059 **Idiomatic**

The verbs in this group are called idiomatic because their meanings cannot be deduced from a simple combination of the pronoun with the infinitive. Consider this contrast:

If you know the meaning of "lever," you can figure out the sentence "Il se lève toujours avant midi."

But knowing "douter" doesn't help much in deciphering "Elle ne se doutait pas de nos intentions," which means "She didn't *suspect* our intentions."

Most of the idiomatic VEEPS are always pronominal. Some do exist in nonpronominal form, where they have different meanings, like **douter** and **se douter.**

There aren't too many verbs in this group, so here are two lists, first those that are always pronominal, then those that have different meanings in their nonpronominal forms:

| *Always:* | *Meaning:* |
|---|---|
| s'écrier | to cry out |
| s'emparer (de) | to seize, grab hold of |
| s'enfuir | to flee, run away |
| s'envoler | to take flight |
| s'évanouir | to faint |
| se fier (à) | to trust |
| se méfier (de) | to mistrust |
| se moquer (de) | to mock, make fun of |
| se repentir (de) | to repent |
| se souvenir (de) | to remember |

*Examples:*
En me voyant, il s'est écrié, "Te voilà, crapule!"
Les colonels veulent s'emparer du gouvernement.
Je me méfie de notre président.
Vous repentez-vous de vos péchés?
Je me souviens d'un incident de ma jeunesse.

Sometimes **se souvenir** is used with an impersonal subject:

Il me souvient d'un incident de ma jeunesse.

| *Different:* | *Meaning:* |
|---|---|
| s'apercevoir (de) | to become aware of |
| apercevoir | to perceive, see |
| s'attendre (à) | to expect |
| attendre | to await |
| se battre (avec) | to fight (with) |
| battre | to beat |
| se douter (de) | to suspect |
| douter (de) | to doubt |
| s'échapper (de) | to get away (from) |
| échapper (à) | to elude |
| se plaindre (de) | to complain (about) |
| plaindre | to pity |

*Examples:*
Le lecteur ne s'attend pas au dénouement.
J'attends avec impatience votre visite.
Tu vas te battre avec le champion vendredi soir.
Pour faire le dessert, elle bat de la crème.
Nous nous plaignons de la chambre malpropre.
Je plains ceux qui tombent dans son piège.

By definition, an idiom is "peculiar to itself within the usage of a given language" (American Heritage Dictionary). Rather than discuss each verb individually, which would both bore you beyond tears and exhaust my modest energies, I suggest you refer to a good dictionary (please, not one of those pocket-sized impostors) for further informative goodies about usage.

There are probably some idiomatic VEEPS that I've overlooked, but this list is close enough to being complete. Learn it. The subjects of all of them should be considered direct objects, so that in compound tenses the participle must agree.

Elles se sont moquées de nous.
Les oiseaux se seraient envolés au son de leurs pas.
On m'a dit que vous vous étiez plaints des repas.
Ma mère ne s'est jamais battue avec sa soeur.

# 7 ○ **Passive**

As distinct from those heard by the Maid of Orléans and from those in singing groups, grammatical voices are neither miraculous nor melodious; they are forms of verbal expression. There are two voices in French: *active* and *passive*.

## 060  ACTIVE VOICE

When you use the active voice, you tell what someone or something did, is doing, or will do. We have all been using it since we were about a year old, and without thinking, "Hmmmmm, I think I'll put this sentence in active form." Here are a few examples of the active voice in English:

> The dish ran away. (*Dish* is the subject; *ran* is what it did.)
> How does your garden grow? (*Garden* is the subject; *grow* is what it does.)
> The little dog laughed. (*Dog* is the subject; *laughed* is what it did.)

## 061  PASSIVE VOICE

That's ludicrously simple, no? Now let's look at the passive voice, which is no less simple. When you use the passive, you designate a person or a thing and then you tell what was done, is being done, or will be done *to* it. Here are a few examples of the passive voice in English:

> The passive voice is explained in this lesson. (*Passive voice* is the subject; *being explained* happens to it.)
> These books were printed in 1503. (*Books* are the subject; *being printed* happened to them.)
> Her contributions will be recognized at the banquet. (*Contributions* are the subject; *being recognized* will happen to them.)

"Why," you ask, "is this guy talking so much about English? We know how to speak English; we're trying to learn French!" I'm glad you asked that. The answer is that in the formation and use of voices, the two languages are very close. Here, for example, are translations into French of the last set of examples:

> La voix passive est expliquée dans cette leçon.
> Ces livres ont été imprimés en 1503.
> Ses contributions seront reconnues au banquet.

062 **Formation of the Passive**

In both English and French, we always use the verb **to be** or **être** in the appropriate tense:

The house *will be* built.
La maison *sera* construite.          Both future

That language *is* spoken in Asia.
Cette langue *est* parlée en Asie.     Both present

The windows *were* opened.
Les fenêtres *ont été* ouvertes.       Both past

We *would be* punished.
Nous *serions* punis.                  Both conditional

The town *had been* destroyed.
La ville *avait été* détruite.         Both pluperfect

The verb **to be** is followed, in both languages, by a participle that indicates the action performed *on*, not *by*, the subject. At the risk of repeating myself, I shall now repeat myself: The French passive is like the English passive, which you know well and use often.

Don't look for trouble. The trick is to become aware of what you do correctly in English without thinking. You will then be able to apply the same process to French.

063  **Tense**

Tense of the passive is an easy matter. Let's try to treat it with the insouciance it so richly deserves. Look at what you do in English:

| *Active:* | *Passive:* |
|---|---|
| Horton *hears* a Who. | A Who *is* heard by Horton. |
| Mine eyes *have seen* the glory. | The glory *has been* seen by my eyes. |
| Jack *built* the house. | The house *was* built by Jack. |

The verb **to be** of the passive is in the same tense as the main verb of the active. In the first example, "hears," present tense, becomes "is," also present tense. In the second, "have seen" becomes "have been," both present perfect. In the third, "built" becomes "was," both past.

French works the same way. To demonstrate this, I shall now execute a stunning tour de force and translate the examples.

| *Active:* | *Passive:* |
|---|---|
| Horton *entend* un Qui. | Un Qui *est* entendu par Horton. |
| Mes yeux *ont vu* la gloire. | La gloire *a été* vue par mes yeux. |
| Jacques *a bâti* la maison. | La maison *a été bâtie* par Jacques. |

Those translations are stylistically horrendous. They are grammatically correct, and they do serve to illustrate the point, but if you accuse me of including them, I'll deny it.

Focusing on another aspect of tense, we can formulate a rule that is completely consistent with what has already been presented. Again, French is just like English:

When the verb **être** is in a compound tense, there are two participles; **été** is always the first of these, just as **been** is always first in the English passive. The main action is expressed in the second participle.

She will have *been kidnaped.*
Elle aura *été enlevée.*
He has *been attacked.*
Il a *été attaqué.*
They had *been expressed.*
Ils avaient *été exprimés.*
Would the ladies have *been shocked?*
Les dames auraient-elles *été choquées?*

### 064  Agreement

You are now emotionally ready to learn of a small complication
in the French passive. You have probably noticed already (look at
the last few examples) that the participle expressing the action
must agree in gender and number with the subject. (See 037 for
more on agreement of participles in the passive.) In this, the participle resembles an adjective, and it follows the same rules. In
those last examples:

*Enlevée,* feminine singular, agrees with the subject *elle.*
*Attaqué,* masculine singular, agrees with the subject *il.*
*Exprimés,* masculine plural, agrees with the subject *ils.*
*Choquées,* feminine plural, agrees with the subject *dames.*

The following paragraph is ingenious, correct, and possibly even
helpful. Its essentials have already been stated; nevertheless . . .

The participle is often used as an adjective. The difference is that
as part of a verb, the participle denotes an activity; as an adjective,
it denotes the state resulting from that activity. Consider the English
sentence "These children are spoiled." Here, the participle "spoiled"
serves a purely adjectival function. But if we say, "These children
are spoiled by their grandparents," we are talking about the
activity, and the sentence is passive. Similarly, in French, "Ces
enfants son gâtés" and "Ces enfants sont gâtés par leurs grands-
parents," or "La porte est fermée" and "La porte est fermée et
rouverte rapidement." See the difference, the shift of emphasis?

### 065  Agent

As you've observed, all these actions we've been talking about
don't just happen; someone or something is responsible for them.

That someone or something is called the agent. Grammatically, the agent may be omitted, which is why the passive is so popular among politicians and generals. They can say things like "It has been decided that . . ." or "Those civilians were sacrificed because . . ." without accepting responsibility.

In English, the agent is expressed after the word **by.** In French it is usually **par** and sometimes **de.** The deciding factor there seems to be whether the main verb denotes an activity or a static condition. However, the deciding factor is not always very decisive; there *is* a little room for confusion. We can't go so far as to say that the two are interchangeable; **par** is much more frequent. In fact, it can be used in almost all cases. There are, however, extremes where a state rather than an activity is clearly indicated, extremes like "La maison est entourée d'arbres," where **par** would be an unlikely choice, giving a little the impression of the trees sneaking up and surrounding the house. It's also pretty clear in such sentences as

> La reine était accompagnée de sa cour.
> Le président est aimé du peuple.

But it's one of those things where only prolonged, profound acquaintance with the language can guarantee 100 percent accuracy. You don't have to do a lot of nail-biting about it. When in doubt, use **par.** Here are some further examples:

> Mon frère a été mordu par notre chien.
> Charlemagne était aimé des douze pairs.
> La pièce avait été louée par les critiques.
> Cette table est couverte de livres.
> Elles sont suivies partout d'un gros caniche.

Here comes another slight complication. Be not dismayed, however; this one reduces, rather than expands, the scope of the French passive.

066 **Subject as Direct Object**

The most important difference between French and English in the use of the passive is this: in French, the verb must be transitive;

it must take a direct object. In other words, the subject must be the direct recipient of the action expressed in the participle. Here are a few English passives that could *not* be expressed with a passive in French:

> She was spoken to.
> You will be sent a package.
> It had never been thought of.
> This glass is often drunk from.

067   The subject in each of those sentences is an *indirect* object. So what can we do with them? Excellent question! The answer is in the use of **on,** a word that appears much more frequently than the American **one.** We can render all the above sentences in the active voice by applying it:

> On lui a parlé.
> On vous enverra un colis.
> On n'y avait jamais pensé.
> On boit souvent dans ce verre.

068   When the agent is expressed, it gets even easier. Take the sentence "She was spoken to." Make her brother the agent. Remember that this sentence can't be passive in French, so instead of saying, "She was spoken to by her brother," we put the agent first, make it the subject, and so transform the sentence into the active voice: "Her brother spoke to her." In this form, it can be said in French, "Son frère lui a parlé." If we add agents to the other three examples, they work the same way.

> You will be sent a package by some friends.
> *can be restated as*
> Some friends will send you a package.
> *which is translatable as*
> Des amis vous enverront un colis.

> It had never been thought of by anyone.
> *can be restated as*
> No one had ever thought of it.
> *which is translatable as*
> Personne n'y avait jamais pensé.

This glass is often drunk from by the workers.
*can be restated as*
The workers often drink from this glass.
*which is translatable as*
Les ouvriers boivent souvent dans ce verre.

069 **Limited Use of the Passive**

Now that you know everything there is to know about the passive, now that you have sacrificed many hours of your precious time to mastering it, I have to tell you that you shouldn't use it much. In neither English nor French is good style very tolerant of the passive. Of course there are times when it is appropriate, even necessary, but try not to overwork it. When either voice will convey your meaning equally well, it is usually wiser to opt for the active.

One place where the passive is required is the science lab report, which is supposed to be colorless and, above all, impersonal:

Four drops of goo *were dripped* into a beaker, which *was heated* to 80 degrees. The resultant glop *was eaten* with a rusty spoon.

And, as I mentioned before, the passive is much favored by politicians and military officials who use it to underplay personal involvement, as in "A hospital was bombed," instead of the more informative "We bombed a hospital."

On that cheerful note, this chapter will be ended.

# 8 ○ **Subjunctive**

070 The subjunctive is not a tense; it is a *mood*. That bears repetition, but I'm not going to write it again. Space is at a premium. Instead, I'll ask you to go back and reread it. Please do that right now. I'll wait.

The official grammatical designation of the subjunctive is a *mood*. Like the indicative, another mood, the one we use most often, the subjunctive has several (though fewer) tenses. We'll get to them.

To recognize the difference between the indicative and the subjunctive moods, keep in mind that the indicative is used to indicate, to point out something that the speaker (or someone else whose opinion is being presented) considers as true, actual, a part of reality, as in the following examples:

> Nous savons que les feuilles sont vertes.
> Je suis sûr qu'il est à la maison.
> Elle va à l'école.
> Tu ne peux pas voler comme les oiseaux.

(Statements of fact may be negative: Nice guys don't come in first. There is no such thing as a free lunch. You can't fly like the birds.)

071 **FUNCTIONS OF THE SUBJUNCTIVE**

The subjunctive serves four major, often interrelated purposes. It shows *doubt, will, judgment, emotion.*

**57**

072 **Doubt**

One important function of the subjunctive is to express things the speaker or the person whose views he represents is not prepared to accept as reality, things he doubts. By using the subjunctive mood, he announces his hesitation. In effect, he says, "Look, I don't really believe this, so don't take it as established fact; don't hold me responsible for its veracity. At best, it's only speculation."

> Nous doutons que les feuilles soient vertes.
> Je ne suis pas sûr qu'il soit à la maison.
> Sa mère ne croit pas qu'elle aille à l'école.
> Il est peu probable que tu puisses voler comme les oiseaux.

Note the difference in feeling between the first and second sets of examples. When we use the subjunctive, we often show an attitude that is dubious or negative.

073 Note also that in the last two examples it was necessary to add whole clauses, to turn the original simple sentence into a subordinate clause. The subjunctive is so named because it is *subjoined*, always part of a subordinate.

In the following sets of examples, each statement will be made three ways: first, in a simple sentence, just as an item of information (remember, the subjunctive doesn't happen in a simple sentence); then as a subordinate in the indicative; and finally, where the main clause expresses doubt or denial, as a subordinate in the subjunctive:

> Vous étudiez trop.
> Je trouve que vous étudiez trop.
> Il est douteux que vous étudiiez trop.
>
> Le prof est fou.
> Il est certain que le prof est fou.
> Je ne pense pas que le prof soit fou.
>
> Le train part à l'heure.
> Il dit que le train part à l'heure.
> Il ne croit pas que le train parte à l'heure.
>
> Nous doutons de son honnêteté.
> Il sait que nous doutons de son honnêteté.

Il refuse de croire que nous doutions de son honnêteté.

074　When using such verbs as **croire** and **penser** in the interrogative, we must remember that the attitude enunciated by the speaker is crucial. Look at this example:

Il est à jeun depuis avant-hier.
Croyez-vous qu'il a (ait) faim?

If you, asking that question, think that "il" must surely be hungry (seems like a good bet), use the indicative. If it is your opinion that he probably isn't hungry, use the subjunctive.

Here's another illustration. The English sentence "Do you think she's tired?" is neutral. There is no reason for choosing either mood over the other in translating it. Now let's put it into a context: "But, Doctor, she slept like a log last night for over ten hours and got up with the brightest eyes I've ever seen. Do you think she's tired?" In this case, the attitude of the questioner must be negative. He would say, "Croyez-vous qu'elle *soit* fatiguée?"

At the other extreme, the context might be something like: "She just finished the Boston Marathon and her face is a lovely robin's-egg blue. Do you think she's tired?" Here the questioner's attitude must be positive. He'd use the indicative: "Croyez-vous qu'elle *est* fatiguée?"

A QUIRK: After "Croyez-vous que . . ." and "Pensez-vous que . . ." we can use either indicative or subjunctive, according to the dictates of context. But after "Est-ce que vous croyez (pensez) que . . ." the subjunctive never appears. Don't forget that languages are nothing but collections of quirks, most of which fall into patterns, thus keeping people like me employed. But I can't make this one fit anywhere. Just learn it. The circumstances that call for the subjunctive remain unchanged. Just don't start a question with "Est-ce que vous croyez (pensez) que . . ." if the subjunctive will follow. Use inversion.

You can say
　　Crois-tu qu'elle est prête?
or

Crois-tu qu'elle soit prête?
but only
Est-ce que tu crois qu'elle est prête?

## .075  Will

Verbs expressing a wish, a desire, a command, are followed by a
subjunctive in the subordinate clause: "Mon père veut que j'*ap-
prenne* le russe." This is a new category, but it shares the basis of
the first. The wish or command suggests that the thing has not
been done yet. In fact, there is room for doubt that it will ever be
done. Like those things in the *doubt* category, it lacks the solid
reality expressed by the indicative. If my father wants me to learn
Russian, then obviously I haven't learned it yet, and it isn't certain
that I'll do his bidding.

In this connection, it is appropriate to bring up an important difference between French and English constructions. This observa-
tion will shed no light on effects of the subjunctive, but it has to
be made and it fits here. The point is:

The only way to express "I want you to . . ." in French is by "Je
veux que vous . . ." followed by a subjunctive. The English construction using the infinitive makes no sense at all in French. Of
course that includes

| | |
|---|---|
| We want them to . . . | Nous voulons qu'ils . . . |
| You want us to . . . | Vous voulez que nous . . . |
| Martha wants George to . . . | Marthe veut que Georges . . . |

Here are a few complete sentences:

Ma mère veut que je réussisse.
Nous souhaitons que vous songiez quelquefois à nous.
J'aime que les choses soient à leur place.

(**Espérer** looks like a shoo-in for a spot in this category, but it
takes the subjunctive only when it is negative or interrogative:
"Nous espérons qu'il viendra." "Espérez-vous qu'il vienne?" "Je
n'espère pas qu'il vienne.")

Word-for-word imitation of the English construction is an atrocity too commonly committed by American students. You may even have been guilty of it yourself. If that is so, I don't want to hear about it. Just promise never to do it again and we'll wipe the slate clean.

We have now studied two of the conditions that require the subjunctive: *doubt* and *will*. There are similarities between them, but they are different enough to require separate headings. Another category, which we will now hang on our belts, fits under the heading of

## 076  Judgment

I refer to those stated in impersonal expressions, following the pattern:

> Il est incroyable que tu aies faim.
> Il est bon que vos étudiiez l'histoire.
> Il est juste que le voleur aille en prison.
> Il est douteux qu'elles sachent l'adresse.

NOTE: The French are less fussy than most American grammars would have us believe about the use of **ce** or **il** as the subject of such sentences. There is an apparent popular tendency in favor of "C'est . . ." Most normative grammarians prefer "Il est . . ." but we must consider that the final vote is not yet in. I recently consulted two highly literate Frenchmen, one of whom insisted on "C'est dommage qu'elle soit si jeune." The other was equally certain of "Il est dommage qu'elle soit si jeune."

Of course, where the subjunctive is concerned, the number of exceptions and of exceptions to the exceptions is even greater than usual. There are irregularities that we can learn only through endless hours of exposure. All I hope to accomplish here is to give you a clear general idea of what the subjunctive does, along with a few rules that will hold up nearly all the time. Behold the following sentences. They are hard to cover with rules, but they do conform to what I have told you about attitudes. In an ideal universe, you would feel the differences.

Il est impossible que tu saches le mot.
Il est possible que tu saches le mot.
Il est peu probable que tu saches le mot.
Il est probable que tu sais le mot.
Il est certain que tu sais le mot.

See that as we move from impossibility through probability to certainty, from a negative to a positive attitude, we switch from subjunctive to indicative.

And look at how much alike these are in spirit:

Je doute que les routes soient praticables. (*doubt*)
Je voudrais que les routes soient praticables. (*will*)
Il est douteux que les routes soient praticables. (*judgment*)

Now in our collection of reasons for the subjunctive we have three major collectibles: *doubt, will,* and *judgment.* The last such category I should like to add can go under the heading of

077  **Emotion**

Emotional reactions, which, unlike the cooler judgments, are expressed in very personal form, also call for the subjunctive. The main clause tells of someone's emotional state and the subordinate, introduced by **que** (as are all subjunctives), gives the reason for that state.

Je suis ravi que vous finissiez.
Il regrette que nous ayons échoué.
Nous ne sommes pas contents qu'elle parte.
Elle est désolée que vous la quittiez.
La cuisinière est très contente que le repas vous plaise.

078  Now there's just one category left: certain conjunctions require the subjunctive. They are:

| Conjunction: | Roughly translatable as: |
|---|---|
| A condition que | On the condition that |
| Afin que | So that |
| A moins que | Unless |
| Avant que | Before |

| Bien que | Although |
|----------|----------|
| De crainte que | For fear that |
| De peur que | For fear that |
| De sorte que | So that |
| Jusqu'à ce que | Until |
| Pour que | So that |
| Pourvu que | Provided that |
| Quoique | Although |
| Sans que | Unless |

Most of these conjunctions can be seen (or squeezed) to fit into one or another of the four categories already established. For example:

> Georges apporte l'echelle pour que Marthe puisse monter sur le toit.
> Abner court pour que Sadie Hawkins ne réussisse pas à l'attraper.

In both of those, something is being done to achieve a certain result. The outcome isn't known, so the speaker can't talk about it with assurance. He can indicate the efforts being made and the *desired* result, but not a fait accompli (that's French). Consider also:

> Je vais rentrer avant qu'il pleuve.
> Je resterai ici jusqu'à ce qu'il pleuve.

In these cases, the rain is anticipated but not actually falling. It may never fall. There is room for doubt.

But that kind of analysis doesn't always work. With **bien que,** for example, it's a total loss:

> Il reste dehors bien qu'il pleuve.

It is definitely raining. Anyone who doubts that is all wet. And this is not a statement of will or a judgment. Perhaps it comes closest to being an emotional reaction. In any case, the verb of the subordinate clause is in the subjunctive. The only way to handle this effectively is to memorize the conjuctions listed. You have four minutes. Go!

That's close to the whole story on the uses of the subjunctive. Only a couple of things remain to be said, and they simplify rather than complicate the picture.

## 079  TENSES

Perhaps you have learned the imperfect and pluperfect subjunctives. Neither of them occurs in conversation or in informal writing. It is most unlikely that you will ever be called on to handle either one actively. Of course you must be able to recognize them in reading, but in normal discourse, the present subjunctive replaces the imperfect, and the passé composé of the subjunctive replaces the pluperfect.

> *Formal:* Je doutais que tu parlasses à la police. (Imperfect subjunctive)
>
> *Informal:* Je doutais que tu parles à la police. (Present subjunctive)
>
> *Formal:* Sa mère regrettait qu'elle fût partie. (Pluperfect subjunctive)
>
> *Informal:* Sa mère regrettait qu'elle soit partie. (Passé composé subjunctive)

I hope your heart is strong; here's yet another bit of good news. There is no future subjunctive. Use the present. There are thus only two tenses of the subjunctive, present and passé composé, that you must be able to use actively.

## 080  AVOIDANCE

Still more tidings of good cheer! Know that the French tend to avoid the subjunctive when there is any easy equivalent. This is commonly the case when the subject in both clauses of a complex sentence would be the same. In English, it is not unusual to say things like

> We are glad that we know the answer.
> I'm sorry that I was born.

In French there would be an infinitive, often (but never with

**vouloir, désirer,** and **souhaiter**) preceded by the preposition **de.**

Nous sommes contents de savoir la réponse.
Je regrette d'être né.

Here are some further examples:

| *English:* | *French:* |
|---|---|
| She isn't sure she has the key. | Elle n'est pas sûre d'avoir la clé. |
| I wish that I were rich. | Je voudrais être riche. |
| You're afraid that you'll fall. | Vous avez peur de tomber. |
| We regret that we must leave. | Nous regrettons de devoir partir. |

# 9 ○ Interrogation

Much of this chapter is laughably easy, but please don't laugh; you just might close your eyes and miss something you didn't know, even about the simplest interrogatives. Enough preamble. Here we go. . . .

081 **INFLECTION**

This is the easiest form of interrogation. Surely you were introduced to it during the first week or two of your first French course. Are you bored yet? Don't go away. Here's something that may prove useful: All spoken questions have special tonal patterns. Those that call for a yes or no answer rise steadily at the end. The simple inflected interrogative differs from all the rest in that the only clue to its interrogativeness is the rising tone (when it is spoken) or the question mark (when it is written). It solicits a yes or no answer.

> Macbeth a tué le roi?
> Ton oncle a les cheveux blancs?
> Billy Pilgrim habitait un abattoir?
> Les chameaux n'ont jamais soif?

082 **INVERSION**

*Inversion* is the interrogative clue present in all other forms. (Of course there's an exception. See 093.)

### 083  N'est-ce Pas?

Ask yourself what is the subject of **n'est-ce pas**. **Ce** is your answer (at least I fervently hope it is). Now ask yourself what is the verb. See? There's an inversion in **n'est-ce pas,** so it turns a statement into a question. It's like adding "isn't she?," "don't they?," and so on. You do it only when you expect agreement.

> Tu m'écriras, n'est-ce pas? (won't you?)
> Elles ont étudié toute la nuit, n'est-ce pas? (didn't they?)
> L'hôtel est agréable, n'est-ce pas? (isn't it?)
> Il pouvait se plaindre, n'est-ce pas? (couldn't he?)
> Ce jeune Mozart a du talent, n'est-ce pas? (hasn't he?)

Literally, **n'est-ce pas?** means "is it not?" Add the word "true" and you see how it works. You make a statement and then add "is it not true?," which has the same effect as "haven't we?," "aren't you?," and so forth.

### 084  Est-ce Que

For a healthful, satisfying, instant question, just start with a cup of hot **est-ce que.** The literal meaning, "is it (true) that . . . ?" converts any statement into a question, but, unlike **n'est-ce pas?, est-ce que** is neutral; it presupposes neither a positive nor a negative response.

Place **est-ce que** immediately before the subject. The inversion (**c'est / est-ce**) is already present, and the statement, with normal declarative word order, becomes a question.

> Est-ce que Napoléon a envahi la Russie?
> Avec combien d'hommes est-ce que Napoléon a envahi la Russie?
> Pourquoi est-ce qu'il a envahi la Russie?
> Est-ce que Candide voulait épouser Cunégonde?
> Quand est-ce qu'il voulait l'épouser?

### 085  Simple Inversion

Otherwise, interrogative inversion is done this way: Simply place the verb before the personal pronoun subject and insert a hyphen between them.

| *Statement:* | *Question:* |
|---|---|
| Il vend la maison. | Vend-il la maison? |
| Elles aiment travailler. | Aiment-elles travailler? |
| Vous apprenez le français. | Apprenez-vous le français? |
| Tu ne comprends pas. | Ne comprends-tu pas? |

The French language is much happier with an alternation of vowel and consonant sounds than with a succession of vowels. Therefore, when inversion brings two vowels together, one at the end of the verb and the other at the beginning of the subject, insert **-t-** between them.

> Trouve-t-il son cheval?
> Va-t-elle en ville?
> A-t-il le temps?

086   SMALL MONKEYWRENCH: When the subject is **je,** don't invert. It is safe to use **est-ce que** or, in informal conversation, simple vocal inflection. Naturally there are exceptions. For instance, there's a series of booklets in French on a variety of subjects. The general title of the series is "Que sais-je?" But I suggest that instead of struggling to learn when this is permissible, you use the universally acceptable **est-ce que.** (See 105.)

> Est-ce que je parle au directeur? (*not* parle-je)
> Est-ce que j'entre? (*not* entre-je)

087   *Word Order with Noun Subject*

When the subject of the interrogative in inverted form is a noun, here, by the numbers, is what you do: (1) noun subject, (2) verb, (3) pronoun doubling noun subject.

> Le téléphone sonne-t-il?
> Les dragons existent-ils?
> La leçon est-elle ennuyeuse?

Here, as always, inversion takes place not with a noun but with a pronoun. One way of thinking about questions like these might be as titles followed by very short compositions. In the first, for instance, the title would be "Le téléphone" and the body of the composition, "sonne-t-il?"

*Word Order with Noun Subject and Interrogative Expression*

Sometimes in an inverted question there will be both an interrogative word or expression and a noun subject. In such cases, place the interrogative words first.

> A quelle heure le téléphone sonne-t-il?
> Où les dragons existent-ils?
> Pourquoi la leçon est-elle ennuyeuse?

088 *Word Order in Compound Tenses*

Remember that for all purposes of placement, the *auxiliary* verb is to be considered *the* verb. Object pronouns come before the auxiliary, negative particles surround the auxiliary, inversion is done with the auxiliary. The participle is tacked on after these operations have been completed.

089 ONE MINUSCULE COMPLICATION: The inverted subject and verb are joined by hyphens. It is an inviolable rule in French that what a hyphen hath joined together, let no man put asunder. See how this affects 3 and 4 below.

1. Quand Mlle Muffet s'est-elle levée?
2. Où le patron t'a-t-il trouvé?
3. En quelle saison la chaleur ne t'a-t-elle pas tourmenté?
4. Pourquoi son père ne les lui avait-il jamais donnés?

In both 3 and 4, the second negative particle is prevented by the inviolable hyphen from taking its normal place right after the auxiliary.

090 **IDENTITY**

To this point, we've been concerned with questions of fact. We've asked whether or not something took place, and why, how, or when it took place. We must also be able to ask the identity of the subject or object: who, what, which.

091 **INTERROGATIVE ADJECTIVES**

**Quel (quels, quelle, quelles)** is an adjective. It must be used with, not in place of, a noun. The effect of interrogative **quel** +

noun is to ask for a choice among possibilities, though often the translation "what" is better than "which." That isn't nearly as clear as I'd like it to be, but I can't come up with a better way to state the case. Just look at these examples:

Quelle heure est-il?
The best *translation,* of course, is "What time is it?"
The *literal meaning*—"Which hour is it?"—asks for a choice.

De quelle couleur sont les roses?
*Translation:* "What color are roses?"
*Literal meaning:* "Of which (choose among them) color are roses?"

The request to make a choice is evident in these French examples:

Quelle robe va-t-elle acheter?
Quelles planètes sont habitées?
Quel métier ton frère apprend-il?      (Note word order
Quels animaux Esope a-t-il décrits?   in these last two.)

Only one verb, **être,** may ever come between **quel** (etc.) and its noun. In such questions, the information asked for is always identity.

Quel est son nom?
Quelle est votre adresse?
Quels sont les jours de la semaine?
Quelles sont les saisons de l'année?

092  DIGRESSION: Well, not really. It's an idiomatic use of **quel** in exclamations like the English "What a ———!" or its plural, "What ———s!" There may be an additional adjective.

Quel homme!
Quelle orthographe atroce!
Quels imbéciles!
Quelles jolies filles!

093  **Interrogative Pronouns**

Let's take **who** first. That's appropriate. As everyone knows, who's on first. This one is easy; whenever you ask the identity of a person, you may use **qui.** And that is true whether the person is subject

(Qui nous appelle?), direct object (Qui cherchez-vous?), or object of a preposition (A qui pense-t-elle?).

One peculiarity must be noted: When **qui** is subject, no inversion is necessary. I think this is the only exception to the statement at 082.

> Qui a tué Cock Robin?
> Qui aimait Iseut la Blonde?
> Qui accompagne l'aveugle Oedipe?

Now **what.** As an interrogative pronoun, **what** may be subject (What made that noise?), direct object (What did you expect?), or indirect object (What are they talking about?).

Indulge me; I'm going to stall a little. Instead of telling you first how to express a thing as interrogative subject, I'll go directly to the direct object. You'll see why soon.

**What** as direct object is **que.** For example:

> Que veut-elle?
> Qu'as-tu fait?

The indirect object (object of preposition) is **quoi.**

> De quoi ont-ils besoin?
> A quoi pensez-vous?
> Avec quoi Jules César écrivait-il? (Note word order.)

The time is now ripe for introduction of the "———est-ce———" device. (We will sell no syntagmeme before its time.)

Note that this device has inversion built in. No further inversion is called for. All four combinations with **qui** and **que** exist:

> Qui est-ce qui . . . ?
> Qui est-ce que . . . ?
> Qu'est-ce qui . . . ?
> Qu'est-ce que . . . ?

***Qui* est-ce *qui*** asks about a *person as subject.*

> Qui est-ce qui frappe à la porte?

Qui est-ce qui sait la réponse?

**Qui est-ce que** asks about a *person as object*, direct or indirect.

Qui est-ce que tu choisis?
A qui est-ce qu'elle doit s'adresser?

**Qu'est-ce que** asks about a *thing as direct object*.

Qu'est-ce que tu veux faire ce soir?
Qu'est-ce que la science révélera la semaine prochaine?

As you may have noticed, all of those have simple, one-word alternatives:

Qui est-ce qui frappe à la porte?
Qui frappe à la porte?

Qui est-ce que tu choisis?
Qui choisis-tu?

Qu'est-ce que tu veux faire ce soir?
Que veux-tu faire ce soir?

I've been holding back the only one that has no simple alternative. There's only one way to start a question about a *thing as subject*: **Qu'est-ce qui.**

Qu'est-ce qui est tombé dans le puits?
Qu'est-ce qui le fait hésiter?

One combination remains: a *thing as indirect object*. The long form for that one is first a preposition, then **quoi,** then **est-ce que,** as in these examples:

Avec quoi est-ce qu'elle l'a battu?
De quoi est-ce que les enfants ont envie?

One-word alternatives for those are:

Avec quoi l'a-t-elle battu?
De quoi les enfants ont-ils envie?

094  *Lequel*

In asking identity, when there is a choice to be made between two or more possibilities, the pronoun to use is a form of **lequel.** It's like saying "which one(s)." **Lequel** (etc.) as an interrogative pronoun may be either subject or object and it may represent any kind of antecedent, human or otherwise.

Laquelle des lettres enverra-t-elle?
Tous les étudiants travaillent. Lesquels réussissent?

Combinations with **a** and **de** are what you might expect:

Nous avons deux chiens; duquel parle-t-il?
Il y a trop de lois. Auxquelles faut-il obéir?

And of course other prepositions may be used.

Voilà les candidats. Pour lequel vas-tu voter?
Je connais vos amies. Chez laquelle passez-vous les vacances?

So ends the chapter on interrogatives. Any questions?

# 10 ∘ Certain Effects of Certain Verbs in Certain Tenses and Moods

This chapter will deal principally with the verbs **devoir, pouvoir, savoir,** and **vouloir.**

## DEVOIR

### 095 Translation and Meaning

Translation is something we must be able to do, but any real understanding must be based on meaning, not on translation, which is often, of stylistic necessity, approximate. Here's what I'm trying (valiantly if not effectively) to get at: We American students are taught to translate **devoir** using "owe," "must," "should have," "had to," or other words, depending on context, and it is entirely fitting and proper that we do so. What we are not reminded of often enough is that for the French, **devoir** is "devoir," that it carries the same freight of connotations with it wherever it goes. "Owe," "ought to," and so on, are words we use in translation to preserve coherence and conciseness in English.

The *meaning* of **devoir,** which does not alter when it alteration finds, has to do with satisfaction of the requirements of logic, reason, and justice; with the rules governing civilized behavior and the proper sequence of events. All of these interrelated connotations are always present. In any individual context, one of them enjoys the full spotlight, but the others are all on stage too, at varying distances from the spot, but still perceptible.

Il me doit cinq dollars.
*Translation:* He owes me five dollars.
*Meaning:* Justice and the rules of civilized behavior require that he pay me five dollars.

Je devrais m'excuser.
*Translation:* I ought to apologize.
*Meaning:* It would be reasonable, logical, and in conformity with the rules of civilized behavior for me to apologize.

096 We may as well stay with the verb **devoir** for now. Without losing sight of its core of meaning, let's look at the different ways in which it must be translated. When it does not have as object the infinitive of another verb, **devoir** is best rendered by the English "to owe."

Combien te doit-il?
Elle lui devait la vie.
Si vous signez le contrat, vous leur devrez la moitié des profits.
Charlemagne devait son empire aux douze pairs.
Où est l'argent que tu me dois?

097 All other uses of **devoir** are with dependent infinitives. Let's take, one at a time, those tenses where the spotlight may shine in unexpected places.

098 **Present**

Nobody should be violently traumatized by the statement that the present of **devoir** is usually best rendered by the English "must" or "have to," expressing either a necessity or a strong probability.

*Necessity*

Je dois faire mes devoirs.
I must (have to) do my homework.

Devez-vous partir si tôt?
Must you (do you have to) leave so early?

Nous devons voir le Louvre.

We must (have to) see the Louvre.

Maintenant les autobus doivent s'arrêter à toutes les intersections.
Now the buses have to stop at all corners.

*Probability*

Le facteur doit avoir ma lettre.
The mailman must have (probably has) my letter.

Vous parlez français? Vous devez être un génie!
You speak French? You must be (probably are) a genius!

Ecris-lui. Elle doit se souvenir de toi.
Write her. She must remember you. (No doubt she remembers
  you.)

Celles qui la suivent doivent être folles.
Those who follow her must be (have got to be) crazy.

Perhaps a little less familiar is the use of **devoir** in the present
tense to indicate the arrangement of events in time. In this application, we translate it as "to be supposed (or scheduled) to . . . "

Tu dois être chez le médecin à une heure.
You are to be at the doctor's at one o'clock.

Quel jour le bateau doit-il partir?
What day is the ship scheduled to leave?

Selon mon calendrier, ils doivent venir ce soir.
According to my calendar, they're supposed to come this evening.

099  **Imperfect**

The same connotations are emphasized as in the present. Here are
some of the same examples in the imperfect.

*Necessity*

Je devais faire mes devoirs.
I had to do my homework.

Deviez-vous partir si tôt?
Did you have to leave so early?

*Probability*

Le facteur devait avoir ma lettre.
The mailman must have had my letter.

Celles qui la suivaient devaient être folles.
Those who followed her must have been crazy.

*Schedule*

Tu devais être chez le médecin à une heure.
You were to be at the doctor's at one o'clock.

Quel jour le bateau devait-il partir?
What day was the ship scheduled to leave?

100 **Passé Composé**

Here again the dominant idea is one of necessity or of probability.
Sometimes, and this is true of the present and the imperfect also,
a single sentence may be enough to tell us which is intended.

*Necessity*

Pour arriver à l'heure hier, j'ai dû courir.
To arrive on time yesterday, I had to run.

Quels bijoux a-t-elle dû vendre pour acheter cet avion?
What jewels did she have to sell to buy that airplane?

*Probability*

Nous avons dû nous tromper de route.
We must have taken the wrong road.

Tu as dû faire sa connaissance hier soir.
You must have met her last night.

But many individual sentences could go either way; that is, they
could emphasize either necessity or probability. "Elle a dû rentrer,"
for instance. We could take that as either "She had to go home"
(necessity) or "She must have gone home" (probability). Fear not,
however. As always, our old dependable rescuer, context, comes
through for us.

*Necessity*

Vous voulez savoir pourquoi elle a dû rentrer avant minuit?
C'est qu'à minuit son splendide carrosse s'est changé en citrouille
et ses chevaux magnifiques en souris.

*Probability*

Je la cherche depuis une heure parmi les autres invités, mais je
ne la trouve pas. Elle a dû rentrer.

As you have probably noticed, both the imperfect and the passé
composé can come across as "had to" and "must have." If you
have any doubts about the differences, please see chapter 4.

## 101  Conditional

Now justice, reason, and the rules for civilized behavior get most
of the light. The conditional of **devoir** expresses a kind of obli-
gation. In the affirmative it tells that something should be happening and suggests that it is not yet happening. In the negative,
something that should not be happening is happening.

Je devrais lui écrire, mais je n'ai pas le temps.
I ought to write him, but I don't have the time.

Le professeur devrait encourager ses étudiants.
The teacher ought to encourage his students.

Vous ne devriez pas fumer tant de cigarettes.
You shouldn't smoke so many cigarettes.

Elle ne devrait pas épouser ce vaurien.
She shouldn't marry that good-for-nothing.

## 102  Conditional Perfect

This is like the conditional, but moved back one step into the past.
In the affirmative, it refers to something that should have happened
but didn't. In the negative, something that should not have happened did.

J'aurais dû lui écrire, mais je n'avais pas le temps.
I should have written him, but I didn't have the time.

Le professeur aurait dû encourager ses étudiants.

The teacher should have encouraged his students.

Vous n'auriez pas dû fumer tant de cigarettes.
You shouldn't have smoked so many cigarettes.

Elle n'aurait pas dû épouser ce vaurien.
She shouldn't have married that good-for-nothing.

So much for **devoir**. Which one would you like to tackle next?
**Pouvoir**? All right; so be it.


## POUVOIR

Not many things here require special attention. One that does is
the difference between the

### 103 Passé Composé and Imperfect

An ability, almost by definition, is continuous. Therefore, when
**pouvoir** refers to the *possession of an ability*, it is much more likely
to be in the imperfect than in the passé composé. The passé composé of **pouvoir** indicates rather the *success or failure of an attempt*.
This is quite consistent with statements made about those tenses
elsewhere in this book (see 033).

Comme j'étais petit, je ne pouvais pas ouvrir la porte.
*Meaning:* Being small, I was unable (for a time, maybe years)
to open the door.

Comme j'étais petit, je n'ai pas pu ouvrir la porte.
*Meaning:* I tried (on a specific occasion) to open the door, but,
being small, I failed.

Nous ne pouvions jamais étudier; il y avait trop de bruit.
*Meaning:* Conditions were never right for studying. There was
always too much noise.

Nous n'avons pas pu étudier; il y avait trop de bruit.
*Meaning:* We gave it a try, but there was too much noise for us
to study.

Don't forget that **pouvoir**, like **devoir**, like all verbs, has its own
set of connotations, unchanging and always present. We must use
a variety of words in English to convey its different emphases.

"Manage to," which suggests success or, in the negative, failure, rather than a continuing ability, is often useful in translating the passé composé of **pouvoir**.

As-tu pu répondre à la dernière question?
Did you manage to answer the last question?

Enfin, j'ai pu parler au premier ministre.
Finally, I managed to speak to the prime minister.

Le pauvre Georges, sans dents, n'a pas pu manger son bifteck.
Poor toothless George couldn't manage to eat his steak.

## Conditional Perfect

of pouvoir is appropriate where English would use **could (might) have** + past participle.

Le pauvre type qu'on a guillotiné n'aurait pas pu être coupable.
The poor guy they guillotined couldn't have been guilty.

Tu aurais pu au moins me téléphoner! Quel fils!
You might at least have phoned me! What a son!

Aurait-il pu lire le journal sans lunettes?
Could he have read the newspaper without glasses?

## Puis

is an alternate form of the first person singular, present tense. It is used when the interrogative is formed without **est-ce que,** by simple inversion. See 086. What I told you there still holds. This is just another one you have to be able to recognize.

Puis-je vous aider, Madame?
May I help you, Madam?

Que puis-je dire pour te convaincre?
What can I say to convince you?

Note that in English, **can** is often used mistakenly instead of **may,** as in, "Can I eat my dessert first, Ma?" This problem does not exist in French, where **pouvoir** serves both purposes.

## SAVOIR

First, an important distinction concerning *ability*. When knowledge, training of the mind, is involved, use **savoir** rather than

**pouvoir** before an infinitive. That makes sense, doesn't it? Often when we say "can" in English, we really mean something like "has the know-how."

His eyes are very weak. I don't think he can read.
(Matter of physical ability. Use **pouvoir**.)
Ses yeux sont très faibles. Je ne crois pas qu'il puisse lire.

The members of that primitive tribe can't read.
(Matter of know-how. Use **savoir**.)
Les membres de cette tribu primitive ne savent pas lire.

I can't write; you took my pencil.
(Physical ability: **pouvoir**.)
Je ne peux pas écrire; tu as pris mon crayon.

She plays the violin well, but she can't play the rebec.
(Know-how: **savoir**.)
Elle joue bien du violon, mais elle ne sait pas jouer du rebec.

In English, the question "Can you swim?" is ambiguous. In French it would be either "Pouvez-vous nager?" or "Savez-vous nager?" The ambiguity disappears.

### 108  Passé Composé and Imperfect

Knowledge, like physical ability, is not an event, not momentary. It is rather a continuing state, and it is therefore expressed in the imperfect rather than in the passé composé. On the other hand, just as **pouvoir** in the passé composé tells of success or failure, **savoir** has to do, in the passé composé, with the acquisition, not the possession, of knowledge.

Comment a-t-elle su qu'il s'appelait Rumpelstiltskin?
How did she *find out?*

En 1975 nous avons su que notre président mentait régulièrement.
We *found out.*

La police n'a jamais su l'identité du coupable.
They never *learned.*

La police ne savait pas qui avait fait le coup.
They *didn't know.*

In the last sentence it's the possession, not the acquisition, of knowledge that is in question. Those are the key words. *Possession* calls for the imperfect, *acquisition* for the passé composé.

**Connaître** follows the same pattern:

Je l'ai connue l'été dernier.
I *met* her last summer.
Elle connaissait mon cousin.
She *knew* my cousin.

### 109 Conditional

It can be straightforward, as in, "Si elle étudiait, elle saurait les réponses," but there is an almost idiomatic use of the conditional of **savoir,** indicating inability, or rather unwillingness, due usually to moral reservations. In direct discourse, the first person is usually involved: **je, nous,** or **on** used as it so often is, as a near equivalent of **nous.** The expression is always negative and **pas** doesn't appear. (I haven't forgotten how foolish it is to say "always." That one just slipped out.)

Je ne saurais accepter un tel cadeau.
*Translation:* I couldn't accept such a gift.
*Meaning* (perhaps): Golly, Mr. Gotrocks, I appreciate the offer, but moral considerations prevent me from accepting it. After all, I'm just your secretary. What would people think, and what strings might, in fact, be attached?

Nous ne saurions supporter ses prétentions.
*Translation:* We can't put up with his pretensions.
*Meaning:* We are unwilling to tolerate his pretensions because we believe that they are morally unjustifiable.

On ne saurait voter contre les mères et la tarte aux pommes.
*Translation:* We couldn't vote against motherhood and apple pie.
*Meaning* (perhaps): Motherhood and apple pie are the cornerstones of our civilization. It would be wicked for us to vote against them.

### 110 Present Subjunctive

An expression equivalent to the English "not that I know of" or "not to my knowledge" is "pas que je sache." It is always (well, you know what I mean) in the first person and always negative.

— Trouve-t-on des perles dans les moules?
— Pas que je sache.

One more notable omission of **pas** is in the mysterious element called "le je ne sais quoi." For instance, pamphleteers of the seventeenth century agreed that one could write a good tragedy by observing the Aristotelian unities plus "bienséance" and "vraisemblance." A great play, however, might be deficient in some of those areas if it possessed that indefinable quality they named "le je ne sais quoi."

## VOULOIR

is a tricky little devil, particularly in the

### 111 Present

The level of insistence, or even of impatience, in "Voulez-vous . . . ?" can vary enormously. It can be a good-humored invitation ("Voulez-vous aller à l'opéra ce soir?"), a mild request ("Monsieur, voulez-vous ouvrir la fenêtre avant la réunion?"), implied criticism ("Mais certainement ils ont perdu le match. Que voulez-vous?"), or an exasperated demand ("Voulez-vous nettoyer votre chambre, petits cochons?"). Overall context and paralinguistic features—tone, facial expression, and gesture—contribute greatly.

### 112

The adverb **bien,** often added to requests and demands, seems to heighten an atmosphere of politeness ("Voulez-vous bien me suivre, Mesdames?") or to intensify the sarcasm of some demands ("Veux-tu bien te taire, imbécile?"). **Bien** is most useful, even necessary, in the affirmative response to an invitation: "Oui, je veux bien."

### 113 Passé Composé and Imperfect

As with other verbs in this chapter (and elsewhere), **vouloir** in the imperfect denotes continuity. There's nothing unexpected about that. The passé composé, also like the others, suggests a moment—in this case, an intention. "Tried to . . . " expresses it pretty well.

Ton chien est méchant. Il a voulu me mordre.
J'ai voulu l'arrêter, mais il courait trop vite.

114  **Conditional**

The special effect of the conditional of **vouloir** is that it softens—
makes less insistent, less harsh—utterances that might be made in
the present indicative. The same is true of English. Only an insen-
sitive clod would say, "I want a pair of clodhoppers" to a clerk in
a shoe store. More civil customers say, "I would like to see a pair
of open-toed, high-heeled, pink clodhoppers." (It really ought to
be *"should* like," but that's a chapter in another book.) Anyway,
"Je voudrais . . ." is the polite, considerate thing to say in French
in such situations. Any time softening of the present indicative is
desired, use the conditional, even when the subject is in the second
or third person.

> La vendeuse lui a demandé, "Qu'est-ce que Monsieur voudrait?"
> Je voudrais encore du pain, s'il vous plaît.
> Voudriez-vous faire partie de notre équipe?
> Garçon, Mademoiselle voudrait une tasse de café.

115  **Conditional Perfect**

With **vouloir,** this is equivalent to "would have liked," sometimes
with the condition stated, sometimes not.

> Elle l'a giflé? Ah, nous aurions voulu voir ça!
> Comment s'appelle cet homme masqué? J'aurais voulu le
>   remercier.
> Si je n'avais pas vu le film, j'aurais bien voulu l'accompagner.

116  **Imperative**

It is certainly possible to imagine other contexts for it, but prac-
tically, the imperative is used in the closing of formal letters; for
instance, "Veuillez, Monsieur, agréer cette expression de mes sen-
timents les plus distingués." Such formulas are quaint antiques,
but they have not yet been discarded. Interestingly, the words are
different in a letter to a woman. It seems that one does not give
ladies orders, so instead of "Veuillez . . ." we find things like "Je
vous prie, Madame, de bien vouloir . . ." It all has about it the
flavor of the eighteenth and nineteenth centuries, when Americans
were still closing letters with "Your obedient servant."

# 11 ○ **Faire, Falloir, S'Agir**

## FAIRE

117 As you may have heard, **faire** appears in an uncommonly wide variety of expressions, in which it may seem to be doing very different things. Here's a sampling of such expressions, with some of the many different words we need to use in English to translate them:

| | |
|---|---|
| Grand'mère a fait un gâteau. | Grandma *made* a cake. |
| Qui fera la vaisselle? | Who will *do* the dishes? |
| J'ai fait une promenade. | I *took* a walk. |
| Il faisait froid. | It *was* cold. |
| Nous ferons de la voile. | We will *go* sailing. |
| Ne fais pas le . . . | Don't *act like* a . . . |
| Il fait bon dormir. | It *feels* good to sleep. |

It isn't hard, however, to find the common thread of meaning that runs through them. It is always a matter of combining the necessary elements and gestures to produce a certain effect. In "Nous ferons de la voile," for example, we are going to manipulate rudder, canvas, ropes, and so on, so that the boat skims over the water. Even in "Il faisait froid" we can see the cold being brought about by a confluence of meteorological phenomena, the work of that ubiquitous insubstantial meddler, the impersonal **il.**

When you are at a loss for a French verbal expression (Come on, admit it, that happens sometimes!), it isn't a bad idea to try inventing one using **faire**. With any luck, you may come up with something at least vaguely Gallic. Remember, "faire l'amour" and "faire la guerre" prove that all's "faire" in love and war.

118   **Causative Faire**

With this turn of phrase, we can talk about having something done:

> They had the house built.

causing something to happen:

> The cold causes the bears to hibernate.

or making someone do something:

> The devil made me do that.

All of those call for the causative **faire** construction in French. The causative construction consists of **faire**, usually conjugated, and the infinitive of the verb expressing what gets done.

> Ils ont fait construire la maison.
> Le froid fait hiverner les ours.
> C'est le diable qui m'a fait faire cela.

We can, without necessarily mentioning an agent, emphasize the event that is brought about:

> Ils ont fait construire la maison. (They caused the construction of the house to take place; they had the house built.)

Or we can give some of that emphasis to the agent, the one who is made to perform the action, as in

> Le froid fait hiverner les ours (where the agents, the bears, are made to hibernate).

119   *Objects*

The thing we cause to be acted on is a direct object:

> Ils ont fait construire la maison.
> Ils l'ont fait construire.

(There are exceptions to all rules, including the one about there being exceptions to all rules. I just realized that the participle in a causative **faire** construction doesn't agree with a preceding direct object. And so it goes.)

The agent, the one(s) made to perform, is a direct object:

> Le froid fait hiverner les ours.
> Le froid les fait hiverner.

"But hold!" you interject smugly, impressed by your own cleverness and delighted by anticipation of my discomfiture, "What if both are in the same sentence?"

First, let me try to make clear to everyone just what you mean.

"Je fais chanter ma fille" is a perfectly good sentence. "Ma fille," according to what I just told you, is a direct object.

So if we replace the noun with a pronoun, the new sentence is "Je la fais chanter." No problem, right? Let's move on.

"Je fais chanter la chanson" is a perfectly good sentence. "La chanson," according to what I just told you, is a direct object. So if we replace the noun with a pronoun, the new sentence is "Je la fais chanter."

See the bind? If both are present, if we want to say, "I make her (my daughter) sing it (the song)," it looks as if we may be stuck with "Je la la fais chanter," which is ridiculous.*

Deliverance from the bind: when both are present, the agent becomes an indirect object. Our ridiculous sentence is now the quite respectable "Je la lui fais chanter."

In noun form, the agent in such cases is object of the preposition à (or sometimes **par**).

> Le professeur fait lire le livre aux étudiants.
> Le patron fait accepter les conditions aux ouvriers.

---

* On peut faire chanter "la la," ou même "la la la la la," mais ça c'est autre chose.

Notre mère faisait faire la vaisselle à ma soeur.
Je fais chanter la chanson à ma fille.

Which permits an ambiguity to get its nose under the tent: are you causing the song to be sung *to* or *by* your daughter? Such double-entendres cause much head-scratching at the annual grammarians' convention, but in reality, context straightens them out.

One more sample: you know that **faire voir** means "to show," and now you know that it can also mean "cause to see," as in "Il a fait voir les aveugles" ("Il a rendu la vue aux aveugles"). The biblical sense of that is quite clear, but imagine that one ophthalmologist is taking another on a tour of his hospital and that he shows him his blind patients . . .

But those are only games. Here's what you must remember:

1. The thing we cause to be acted on is direct object of a causative **faire** construction.

   Tu feras réparer *la voiture.*
   Tu *la* feras réparer.

   Le conservateur a fait restaurer *le tableau.*
   Le conservateur *l'*a fait restaurer.

2. The agent, the one(s) made to act, *may be* the direct object of a causative **faire** construction.

   Ce poète fait penser *les critiques.*
   Ce poète *les* fait penser.

   Tu ne peux pas faire boire *ton cheval.*
   Tu ne peux pas *le* faire boire.

3. When both the agent and the thing he is made to act on are expressed, the agent becomes an indirect object.

   Tu *lui* feras écrire la lettre.
   Tu la *lui* feras écrire.

   Je *leur* fais réciter la leçon.
   Je la *leur* fais réciter.

120  *Word Order*

You have noticed the order, haven't you? Pronoun objects come immediately before (or, in the affirmative imperative, immediately after) **faire.**

> Nous les faisons attendre.
> Faisons-les attendre.

> Vous la faites pleurer.
> Ne la faites plus pleurer. (Negative imperative)

Noun objects come after the second verb, usually the direct followed by the indirect.

> Il fait suivre sa femme par un détective privé.
> On fait enlever les bonbons aux enfants.

And of course there are combinations of noun and pronoun objects.

> Il la fait suivre par un détective privé.
> Il lui fait suivre sa femme.

> On les fait enlever aux enfants.
> On leur fait enlever les bonbons.

121  *Agreement*

The participle of **faire** in a causative construction is invariable. Use the basic masculine singular form.

> Les pommes? Le magicien les a fait disparaître.
> Où est la tasse que j'ai fait remplir?

122  *Reflexives*

When the second verb in a causative construction is pronominal, omit the reflexive pronoun.

> Elle fait coucher ses enfants de bonne heure.
> Une mauvaise carte m'a fait tromper de route.
> Cette actrice le faisait souvenir de sa dixième femme.

123  **FALLOIR**

Don't be offended; there are many otherwise quite honorable and even articulate people who forget about the negative of **falloir.** That's why I feel constrained to include this reminder.

As we'd expect, "Il est nécessaire" means "It is necessary" and "Il n'est pas nécessaire" means "It is not necessary."

But **falloir** doesn't work quite that same way. "Il faut que je . . ." means "I must . . . ," but "Il ne faut pas que je . . . " carries an interdiction. Instead of "I don't have to . . . ," it means "I *must not* . . . " That's what takes a little getting used to.

Il faut que vous parliez.
You must speak.

Il ne faut pas que vous parliez.
You must not speak.

Il fallait qu'elle sache la vérité.
She had to know the truth.

Il ne fallait pas qu'elle sache la vérité. She couldn't (it was necessary that she not) know the truth.

## 124  S'AGIR

Again, just a brief reminder. Please don't forget that though **agir** may have a first-, second-, or third-person subject, as in

La police agit vite pour surprendre les malfaiteurs.
Si tu n'agis pas ce matin, tu vas perdre l'occasion.
Il me semble que nous avons agi inconsidérément.

its pronominal form, **s'agir,** works only with the impersonal **il,** as in

De quoi s'agit-il?
Dans cette fantaisie, il s'agit d'un prof sympathique.
Il s'agissait de lui passer un coup de fil.

You may find this hard to believe, but once in a while a student trying to say something like "The lecture was about . . . " uses **s'agir** with "la conférence" as its subject. You wouldn't ever do anything remotely resembling that, would you?

# 12 ○ Time

The time has come.
　　　　　　　　　—Walrus

If time flies, then where's my bowling ball?
　　　　　　　　　—Anonymous

This will not be an encyclopedic presentation of the French expressions dealing with time. All I want to do is go over and perhaps clarify some of the things that have given my students the most trouble.

First, let's try to put behind us the matter of

## 125　TEMPS

Le temps (when it is not the weather) is that dimension through which we are all traveling on our way to the crepuscular zone. The word refers to slices of that dimension or sometimes to the concept as a whole.

　　*Les Temps modernes* (a magazine)
　　Je n'ai pas le temps.
　　Je descendrai dans une minute; le temps de me peigner.
　　Le temps n'attend personne.

Hardly ever is a number used with the word. That's because it refers to an *amount* of something rather than to one or more things.

126   An item has just occurred to me that is perhaps unworthy of our attention, so maybe you'd best pay no mind to the rest of this paragraph. Sometimes students, no doubt under the malign influence of diabolical forces that they have conjured forth by playing certain rock records backward, try to translate word for word the English expression "to have a good time." The result is horrendously bad French. Remember **s'amuser.** And while I'm in the

127   trivia department, don't forget not to use an article with the word **longtemps.** All by itself, it is "*a* long time" or even "*for a* long time."

Okay, you may come back now. Time for us to take a look at

128  **FOIS**

**Fois** is not a slice of time; it is rather a crumb fallen from that slice. Here's another equally so-so metaphor: If **temps** is a tornado, then **fois** is where it touches down. It is like the English word **occasion** as used in such expressions as "on several occasions." **Fois** is a noun, but (this just struck me and it may be helpful) it is used almost exclusively in adverbial expressions rather than as subject or object of a verb.

(There are missing tape recordings proving that the following dialogue never took place.)

— Tu vas passer l'examen encore une fois?
— Oui, et cette fois-ci je ne vais pas le rater.
— Combien de fois as-tu essayé?
— Une vingtaine de fois.

Some further examples:

Nous nous sommes rencontrés une fois en Turquie.
Cette fois-là elles sont tombées.
J'ai vu ce film au moins dix fois.

**Fois** is also used in multiplication:

809,56 fois 13,552 font 10.971,157.
(Three cheers for the calculator!)

129 **AVANT DE, APRES AVOIR**

"Before ——ing" is **avant de** + infinitive.

Avant de manger, il faut se laver les mains.

"After ——ing" is so much like "before ——ing" in English that there is a strong temptation to try the same thing in French. Resist! The only way to say "after ——ing" in French is **après avoir** + past participle.

Après avoir mangé, il faut se laver les dents.

Don't forget to use **être** as the auxiliary when it is called for, as in

Après s'être lavé les mains, il a mangé.
Après être entré, j'avais refermé la porte.

See how the sequence of events remains the same in each of the following sets of three sentences:

Je lis un chapitre et puis je m'endors.
Après avoir lu un chapitre, je m'endors.
Avant de m'endormir, je lis un chapitre.

Il finit son travail et puis il rentre chez lui.
Après avoir fini son travail, il rentre chez lui.
Avant de rentrer chez lui, il finit son travail.

130 **DEPUIS**

For those of us who are less than completely bilingual, there is no progressive tense in French. We use progressives a lot in English; they are made up of the auxiliary **to be** and the present participle.

Look, Ma, I'm dancing.
I've been dancing for years.
She was studying.
She'd been studying for hours.

It is quite obvious in the first and third of those that the dancing is going on and that the studying was going on. To talk about things that *are going on now,* French uses the simple present tense; for things that *were going on then,* the simple imperfect. It may be a little less obvious, but in order for me to say "I've been dancing for years," I must still be dancing. Similarly, if she had been studying for hours, then she was still studying. Here too, French calls for the simple present and the simple imperfect:

> Regarde, Maman, je danse.
> Je danse depuis des années.
>
> Elle étudiait.
> Elle étudiait depuis des heures.

**Depuis** . . . refers to the elapsed time or to be starting point. It is used both in asking and in answering the questions "How long . . . ?" and "Since when . . . ?"

> *Elapsed time:*
> Depuis combien de temps dansez-vous?
> Je danse depuis des années.
>
> *Starting point:*
> Depuis quand dansez-vous?
> Je danse depuis 1980.
>
> *Elapsed time:*
> Depuis combien de temps étudiait-elle?
> Elle étudiait depuis longtemps.
>
> *Starting point:*
> Depuis quand étudiait-elle?
> Elle étudiait depuis midi.

131  **IL Y A (AVAIT) AND VOILA**

**Il y a** can be used to ask and to answer the question of elapsed time:

> Combien de temps y a-t-il que tu bois?
> Il y a des mois que je bois.
>
> Combien de temps y avait-il que vous voyagiez?
> Il y avait quinze jours que nous voyagions.

But it can neither ask nor answer the question of starting point. Only **depuis** can fill that job. **Il y a** followed by an indication of elapsed time does function just like the English **ago.**

Je suis arrivé il y a un mois.
Nous avions déjeuné il y avait trois heures.

**Voilà,** with just one very familiar substandard exception that I know of,* can be used temporally only to make a statement about duration.

Voilà deux siècles que le roi est mort.
Voilà des mois qu'il pleut sans cesse.

132    **——ANT AND ETRE EN TRAIN DE**

Nothing is better calculated to drive a French teacher out of his gourd (or whatever the current slang is) than direct translation into Franglais of progressive tenses. French does offer a present participle, the form in ——**ant.** (Once again I must admit that long-time perfectly fluent speakers seem able to use it without violating any taboos in sentences like "Elle était mangeant . . . " The thing is fraught with peril for us ordinary mortals, however, and I must recommend that you avoid it.) Often it occurs, correctly, with the preposition **en.** The phrase formed is much like the English **while, by,** or **upon** ——**ing,** depending, of course, on context. Examples are:

En traversant la mer dans sa baignoire, il a lu Proust. (*while*)
Je jouerai du violon en attendant ton retour. (*while*)

Elle amusait les enfants en faisant des grimaces. (*by*)
M. Tucker paie son souper en chantant. (*by*)

En touchant le fil, j'ai reçu un choc. (*upon*)
Elle sourit en se souvenant de sa jeunesse. (*upon*)

When there is anything unusual, incongruous, or surprising about the two things going on at the same time, use **tout en.**

---

*Voilà-t-il pas une heure de perdue? (Isn't that a wasted hour?)

Dagwood boit du café tout en nouant sa cravate.
Il nous parlait de la moralité tout en nous volant.
Les écoliers font leurs devoirs tout en regardant la télé.
Elle joue aux échecs tout en écrivant des lettres.
Il siffle très fort tout en mangeant des biscuits.

133   When you want to express the immediacy suggested in the English
progressive tenses, use the expression **être en train de** + infinitive.

Je n'ai rien entendu. J'étais en train de me laver les oreilles.
Nous sommes en train de dîner. Ce n'est pas le moment de parler
de ça.

134   **JUSQU'A CE QUE**

Several prepositions become conjunctions just with the addition
of **que.** Among them are the temporal **avant, après, depuis,** and
**pendant,** as in these examples:

Avant la guerre, il habitait la ville. (preposition)
Il voulait déménager avant que la guerre n'éclate. (conjunction)

Elle reviendra après les vacances. (preposition)
Elle reviendra après que les vacances se terminent. (conjunction)

135   Come to think of it, that doesn't help you much unless you know
what prepositions and conjunctions are. Prepositions are those
(usually) little words that indicate relations, often spatial or temporal. **Chez, dans, devant,** and the few mentioned above fit that
description. Among those that don't are **pour, malgré,** and
**comme.** Prepositions are followed by their substantive objects.

Qu'est-ce qu'il y a dans la boîte?
Le petit garçon court vers elle.

With a few exceptions (so what else is new?), conjunctions link
two clauses. Each clause has its own subject and verb, so a conjunction must be followed by at least those two items.

La cigale chantait pendant que le soleil brillait.
Elle chantait tandis que la fourmi travaillait.

**Jusqu'à** is a preposition and its corresponding conjunction is **jusqu'à ce que.** The preposition, but not the conjunction, works in both time and space.

> Je cours du matin jusqu'au soir.
> Ils vont prendre le bateau. Nous les accompagnons jusqu'au Havre.

Students seem to have some difficulty with the conjunction **jusqu'à ce que.** Because of the special relationship that exists between us, I wanted to be sure you have it under control. The difficulty probably arises because the English **until** is both a preposition and a conjunction.

Here are a few examples of the conjunction **jusqu'à ce que.** Remember that it works in time only and that it requires the subjunctive. (See 078.)

> Ces ours vont dormir jusqu'à ce que la neige disparaisse.
> Nous attendrons jusqu'à ce que l'autobus vienne.
> Tais-toi jusqu'à ce que je te demande ton avis.

## 136  PENDANT AND POUR

Some of our misguided countrymen try to get away with using **pour** in *all* the temporal expressions where **for** serves in English. The reality is far from that simple, alas. I've just spent a couple of hours devising, checking, and rejecting guidelines for the use of **pendant** and **pour** as prepositions indicating an extent of time. The matter is fiendishly complex. Here are a couple of things that hold true often enough not to be hopelessly misleading:

Use **pendant** any time the word **during** would fit.

> Qu'avez-vous fait pendant la panne d'électricité?
> Pendant les vacances, il a fait le tour du monde.

Otherwise, use **pour** mainly to indicate a look ahead. This may be in the past, present, or future.

Je suis allé à Paris pour mon dernier semestre.
Ou vas-tu pour les vacances?

**Pour** always indicates the entirety of the time period specified after it. **Pendant** may indicate a part of that time. Look at the first of the two examples above. As it stands, it means that I went to Paris for the whole of my last semester; but if we replace **pour** with **pendant,** it can mean that I spent a part of my last semester in Paris, that I went there *during* (not necessarily for all of) that semester.

I could go on and on, giving you special cases and partial rules (or roulettes), but in the absence of any mighty unifying principle, that would be counterproductive. If you learn what's here, you should be safe from accusations of illiteracy.

And that seems to be a fitting last sentence for this book.

# Index

(References are to the three-digit numbers that appear in the margins of the text.)